PORTRAIT OF THE THAMES

(From Teddington to the Source)

Portrait of
THE THAMES

(From Teddington to the Source)

J. H. B. PEEL

ILLUSTRATED
AND WITH MAPS

ROBERT HALE · LONDON

First Edition 1967
Reprinted 1969
Reprinted 1976

ISBN 0 7091 0748 X

Robert Hale & Company
Clerkenwell House
Clerkenwell Green
London, EC1R 0HT

Printed in Great Britain by
Lowe & Brydone (Printers) Ltd, Thetford, Norfolk

This book is dedicated to
GILLIE POTTER
famous for his knowledge
and love of England

The Thames is liquid history.

JOHN BURN

CONTENTS

ILLUSTRATIONS

MAPS

The photographs for this book were taken by J. H. B. Peel

I

BON VOYAGE

ALL portraits are self-portraits. Not even a physicist can elude his own personality. This portrait, certainly, does not try to achieve a spurious detachment. Let us allow, therefore, that we are two men in a boat; or, if you prefer, that you have hired me to be your pilot. And since a pilot is expected to show his credentials, I shall state my own, in one sentence. I first saw the Thames more than sixty years ago; for thirty-five years I lived in the Chiltern Hills through which it flows; on foot or by boat I have travelled the voyage that we are about to make—not solely for this occasion but many times, at all seasons, in every weather, by day and at night.

A pilot, of course, is not required to coerce the passengers nor to harry the crew. He will fulfil his function if he states what he knows to be true and what he believes to be probable, thereafter offering his own analysis of the situation. A modicum of courtesy and good humour can make the voyage seem memorable; and at the end of it, perhaps, we shall be glad that we have travelled in each other's company.

The Thames bears the brunt of English history. The Tower of London, Whitehall, Windsor Castle, Hampton Court, Runnymede, the great houses flanking the upper reaches, Oxford itself (a home of Parliaments and Kings) . . . these felt the very pulse of England, for the river in those years broadcast a news-bulletin to a large part of the more important half of the kingdom; and some of its despatches came full-sail from Moscow and Pekin. The portrait, in short, assumes an international chiaroscuro, but without ever obscuring the fact that the Thames, which is utterly English, belongs to the whole of Britain. To follow its course will prove exciting, and may appear somewhat as a duty to every Englishman who would accept Sir Thomas Browne's advice: "Be not an alien in thine own land."

13

Our own land, alas, tends to alienate us from its climate, which is unfortunate because a voyage on the Thames pleads for fine weather, as Edmund Spenser pleaded, four centuries ago, when he besought the Sun:

> Do not thy servant's simple boon refuse;
> But let this day, let this one day, be mine;
> Let all the rest be thine.
> Then I thy sovereign praises loud will sing,
> That all the woods shall answer, and their echo ring.

Summers now are as English as they were then, yet in one respect we have an advantage over Spenser; weather forecasts tell us when we may enjoy a sunny day. In another respect Spenser had an advantage over us, for whereas in his time a sunny day made no great difference to the traffic, in our time a sunny day evokes a plague of gnats. Except during the early morning, or after dark, summer is not the best season for savouring the Thames, at any rate below Oxford. On a fine day between June and September you may have to queue at the locks, endure jazz from the banks, and maintain constant watch against the watermanship of Britons who, so far from ruling the waves, are defeated by a tideless backwater. It is a hard saying, but worthy to be repeated; a summer voyage in search of the Thames too often defeats its own purpose.

That leaves spring, autumn, winter; and which of them excels the rest is a matter of temperament and mood. In May, when the leaves have come out to play, the river is at its gayest; in October, when the visitors have gone in to work, the river is at its gaudiest; throughout the winter it attains the astringency of a poet who, in his age, has pared away the rind of ornament, to bare the kernel's core.

Sir Thomas Browne (he will bear a second citation) coined a phrase—"the whole alphabet of man"—which can be applied to the Thames itself; but instead of following its course from A to Z, we shall commence near the end because, after all, the beginning is not necessarily the best place from which to start. By working up-river, out of London, and into the country, we can track the Thames to its source 143 miles from Teddington. That way, I suggest, the voyage will seem more like a holiday. Even the staunchest townsman must agree that the Cotswolds are a destination more desirable than Battersea power-house.

One other point seems worth emphasizing. A portrait of the Thames is something more than the likeness of a river or of a region; it is the panorama of a people, the English people, that hybrid entity gotten of Goth and of Celt, of Roman and of Saxon, of Viking and of Norman; for nearly a thousand years a proud people, a national people, whom no enemy has yet invaded; but now at last and for the first time so less than proud that it has become ashamed of its own nationhood. A man nowadays may cry for this or that far country, even although the country be no friend of his own; but for England and St. George he may not cry, unless he would be reviled and mocked as a voice crying in the wilderness of archaic and imperial pretence. This perversion of the nature of love may pass. Meanwhile, though it is sweet and well-becomes a man to die for his country, it is sweeter and not less decorous to live for it, to be proud of it, to delight in it. Perhaps this portrait will kindle or rekindle in those who read it that love of England which is based upon a knowledge of the facts; for indeed it is no small thing to have been born in England, to have compared her merits and defects with those of other nations, to have wandered the length and breadth of her land, and to have discovered that neither Time nor custom shall cloy such infinite variety.

Our own sailing orders contain two provisos.

First, we shall limit the voyage; starting from Teddington Lock, and ending at the source in a meadow near Cirencester, with only a backward glance at the lower reaches. To explore the Pool and the Port, as well as the upper river, would be to swallow more than we could comfortably drink. The choice of Teddington was not haphazard. Above Teddington begins the jurisdiction of the Thames River Authority, formerly Thames Conservancy Board; below Teddington the Port of London Authority takes over. Portraiture must at that point give way to draughtsmanship.

Second, we shall try always for a portrait, never for a snapshot. When Defoe published some cursory notes on parts of the Thames two centuries ago, he assured his readers: ". . . I shall speak of the river as it really is . . . made glorious by the splendor of its shores, gilded with noble palaces, strong fortifications, large hospitals, and publick buildings . . . made famous by the opulence of its merchants . . . and by the inumerable fleets of ships upon it, to and from all parts of the world." That was an admirable recipe, which many gazetteers have kept up-to-date. Historic places and events do indeed form part of the portrait, especially between Teddington and Windsor, where not a great deal else exists to be described; but the Thames is more than its noble palaces, more than its large hospitals, more than the opulence of its merchants. The Thames includes sunlight on Cliveden Reach, starlight over Quarry Wood, and Lechlade through a mist. The Thames means an old man leaning on a gate at Bisham, and a young girl swimming from a launch at Sonning. The Thames is the ripple of water through your fingers, the grip of the grass when you step ashore, the call of a cow at milking time.

The Thames, in short, offers more than history, more than architecture, more than commerce and flora and fauna. The Thames exceeds the sum of its parts. There lies the rub—and there, if we can find it, the reward.

Cul-de-sac at Great Marlow

THAMES CONSERVANCY

NOTICE

ALL PERSONS USING THE RIVER THAMES AND THE LOCKS. WORKS. AND TOWING PATHS THEREOF MUST TAKE THEM AS THEY FIND THEM. AND DO SO AT THEIR OWN RISK.

BY ORDER.

GLANCING ASTERN: LONDON RIVER

To begin a voyage by glancing astern may suggest a poor spirit of adventure. Sailors, however, always take their bearings before casting-off; and at Teddington you cannot profitably peer ahead until you have briefly glanced behind, because Teddington symbolizes a parting of the ways. Above Teddington, the Thames starts to become a stream; below Teddington, it begins to be an estuary. Here, too, the tidal meet the non-tidal waters. What lies astern is new, commercial, measurably tinged with brine; it is urban and international. What waits ahead is old, pastoral, without trace of salt water; it is rural and English.

What, then, does lie behind? What is it that we are leaving, yet shall meet in embryo throughout the voyage? It is the largest harbour in the world; and John Masefield has evoked it from two lines:

> The great street paved with water, filled with shipping,
> And all the world's flags flying, and the seagulls dipping.

Nor is that shipping confined to Tilbury or Gravesend. Even at Teddington the tugs and barges ply for hire—those outriders from the ocean-going vessels bringing their spices and their timber, the ore and the oil, the "sandalwood, cedarwood, and sweet white wine". And the further you range in imagination, the closer comes the sea. Ships larger than the classic *Mayflower* put in at Hammersmith, sometimes through waves so high that they will sink a Boat Race. From Tower Bridge the stockbrokers and their typists may overhear a dozen foreign languages, each chanting its own maritime *patois* (not always politely). Lower yet, and you will sight some of the world's biggest liners.

No one knows when a vessel first ventured on the Thames, but in Caesar's day Londinium was already a flourishing harbour, well

You have been warned!

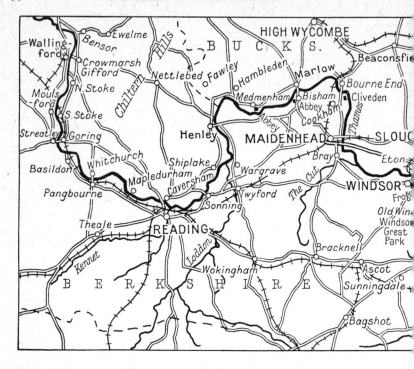

sited to trade with the Continent. When Elizabeth I became Queen
the masts were bristling from Tilbury to the Tower. When Anne
became Queen the Port of London was handling some 65 per cent
of the kingdom's export and import trade. Even during the reign
of Charles I a certain John Taylor, commonly called the Water
Poet, reckoned that "the number of watermen and them that lived
and were maintained by them could not be less than 40,000".
That was certainly an exaggeration, but it does emphasize the
importance of river traffic. Moreover in John Taylor's day the
medieval concept of a just price (or reasonable profit) had faded
from the national consciousness, and was replaced by *laissez-faire*
or do-as-you-like. The Fathers of the Church never were able to
civilize Mammon, but they did contrive to tame it by pointing
a middle way between Communism and unrestricted private
enterprise. When that middle way was dismissed as romanticism,
every man felt free to grab whatever he could. The livery companies, it is true, continued to uphold standards of craftsmanship

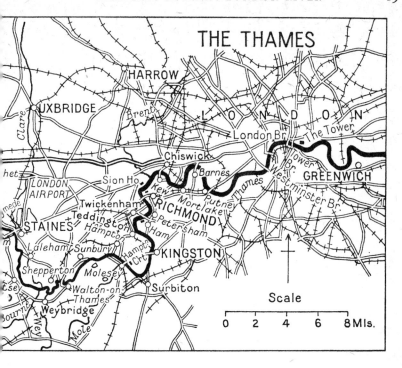

and integrity, but what we now call labour relations so deterior-
ated that dockland feuds between master and men were as bitter
then as they are today. The history of the Port of London is a
litany of battles between, on the one hand, the dock owners and,
on the other, the lightermen and wharfingers who used the quays
but claimed to be exempt from contributing toward their upkeep.
Such uncivil war caused chaos and congestion. As late as the
nineteenth century a ship's purser wrote: "An adverse wind will
drop, but God knows whether any wind at all shall ever shift us
through the mass of shipping above Gravesend." Yet the picture
was not wholly black. In 1800, for example, it took more than a
week to unload and reload a ship of 500 tons, but in 1862 ships of
4,000 tons were being turned round in six days.

Even so, the congestion and incompetence continued to increase, and by the beginning of the twentieth century they were
jeopardizing London's pre-eminence over her medieval rivals.
A Royal Commission, therefore, was required to prescribe

remedies. These were drastic. In 1909 the era of wholly private enterprise ended and was replaced by the Port of London Authority, which describes itself as a "statutory undertaking independent of Government or municipal control . . . designed to be representative of all users of the Port". Ten members of the Authority are appointed by the Greater London Council, two by the Corporation of the City of London, two by the Ministry of Transport, and one each by the Admiralty and the Corporation of Trinity House. Of the elected members, eight represent shipowners, eight the merchants, and one each of the wharfingers and owners of river craft. The chairman and vice-chairman are elected by the Board, sometimes from within itself, sometimes from without. The Board is reconstructed every three years.

In 1974 the Port Authority controlled a dock area of more than 1600 acres offering berths along twenty-two miles of deep water quays below Teddington. Two famous docks, the London and the Surrey Commercial Docks have closed and the Saint Katherine Dock is now leased out by the G.L.C. as a yachting area. The India Docks (opened in 1806) have amalgamated with the Millwall Docks (1868) and the Victoria Dock (1835) with the Royal Albert Dock (1880) and the George V Dock as the Royal Docks; the Tilbury Dock has been considerably extended. In 1974 the Port handled 51.51 million tons of goods and accepted 21.4 million net tons of external shipping.

Most of this traffic remains below Tower Bridge, which can be raised and lowered for the passage of large ships (and during the late war, when I served awhile with the Royal Naval Auxiliary Patrol, one of my more enjoyable duties was, on occasion, to order the lowering and raising). The only sizeable ships plying above London Bridge are colliers that serve the various gas and electricity stations. These vessels have a low superstructure and collapsible funnels which allow them to pass under the bridges.

The concentration of shipping below Tower Bridge is relatively modern. The vicar of Bray smoked tobacco that came by water; Pope at Twickenham sipped tea that came by water; Carlyle in Chelsea belched before a fire of coals that came by water; and water carried corn from Cricklade to Camberwell. The decay of this up-river traffic began with the invention of steam locomotives, and ended with the arrival of motor-cars. We can no longer say what Defoe reported: "The Thames . . . is the channel for conveying an infinite quantity of possessions from remote countries to London, and enriching the counties again that lye near it, by the return of wealth and trade from the city. . . ."

On our own voyage we shall pass many villages and small country towns that were once inland harbours, supplying the countryside with commodities from London, and London with commodities from the countryside. Old men alive can remember the years when barges travelled as far as Lechlade. Today that up-river traffic has disappeared.

Passenger craft, however, continue to ply a brisk trade on London River. Indeed, the P.L.A. provides sightseeing cruises between Tower Pier and the docks. In 1974 more than 20,000 passengers travelled in these P.L.A. launches.

London River is the headquarters of the senior Division of the Royal Naval Reserve, which has two ships moored near Blackfriars Bridge. History repeats itself, and is seen to repeat itself, so often that one wonders why any historian should bother to deny the fact. For example, another of my inconspicuous wartime tasks was to scour the Thames for any craft which seemed suitable to take part in the Dunkirk epic. Five centuries before that, on 1st November, 1462, John Paston's agent, writing from London, sent news of a similar commandeering for the war against France: ". . . there were arrested by the Treasurer forty ships lying in the Thames, where of many small ships; and it is said to carry men to Calais, in all haste for fear of the King of France. . . ."

London River (that is, the Thames between Teddington and the Estuary) differs greatly from London's River (the Thames between Teddington and Windsor). London River is a world of which the average Londoner knows scarcely anything at all, and the average Englishman even less. It is an amphibious world of deep-sea sailors and longshore-men. It is a world wherein Chinamen and Swedes mingle with Russians and Malays. It is a world of wits, as any man knows who has lived in it long enough and well enough to have been accepted by it. As master of the pat repartee, the Cockney has no peer. Beside him, the cocktail *raconteur* seems as contrived as a booby trap, and not less feline.

In short, London River is—as Shakespeare said of England— a world in itself. And if a portrait of it were required in music, then the finale of Holst's Jupiter suite would offer a notable likeness; the chords rising and falling with the tide, with the sea itself, whose invisible presence is proven by Masefield's "dirty British coaster with a salt-caked smoke-stack", belching her way past Tilbury, past Wapping, past the Tower, there to drop anchor within a cable's length of Wren's cathedral.

That, in miniature, is London River, and although its substance falls astern, its spirit will remain as an intangible fellow-passenger —a memory of rope and tar and rust-red rivets, and of the immemorial music of the sea.

Our own port of embarkation is the largest lock in the river, built in 1904 especially to take tugs and a line of barges: Teddington Lock.

III

LONDON'S RIVER: TEDDINGTON TO WINDSOR

THE beginnings of London's River are less impressive than some could wish, yet more auspicious than many suppose. Here a long and furious weir composes its own water music. On the left bank, dwarfed by modern buildings, Ferry Road has several endearing Victorian cottages, slaked by a pub, the "Tide End Cottage", whose name announces a fact. Ahead, the river runs a gauntlet of trees. Simply to be among those trees, and on the water, evokes a mood of rural seamanship. They will remain constant fellow-travellers, both mile-posts and calendars. No matter what happens—and there are some eyesores to be confronted—they at least will never desert a dispirited ship. Even at industrial Reading they abide, stalwart as sleepless sentries, doing their blessedest to shame what they cannot conceal. But appearances may be deceptive. In 1906 this placid, almost turgid, river was so fiercely in spate that it swept a tug over Teddington Lock.

The name Teddington means "the home of Tudda's people" —Tudda having been a local headman—and in the year 969 it was spelled Tudintun. Philologists used to believe that the word meant "the place where the tide begins". Their hypothesis seems plausible, but is invalid because "tide" never was the Old English word for tide.

Here, then, at the home of Tudda's people, our boat is launched, and we ourselves make ready for a voyage into the unknown; bearing in mind that a portrait, unlike a photograph, cannot be conjured up in a trice. Its creation is an accretion, taking time; and if the preliminary strokes resemble a series of disjointed daubs, it is because this reach of the river lacks the one element—the human element—that can truly bring it to modern life. There are hundreds of thousands of people here, but no riverfolk. Only in deep country will still-life become a portrait.

Even so, this is not a reach to be skimmed. On the contrary, it is the most heavily marked by great events and famous men. William Penn lived at Teddington before he sailed to found Pennsylvania. And here, during the last two years of his life, sauntered a man who, having lived and died unknown, suddenly achieved lasting renown. The story is literally a detective story, perhaps the most amazing of its kind. What happened was as follows.

In 1896 a certain William T. Brooke is browsing through a second-hand bookstall when he comes across two anonymous manuscript volumes of poetry. Being a scholar, he has only to read a couple of pages in order to perceive that he has stumbled on the work of a genius. For a few pence Brooke buys the manuscripts that today would fetch a fortune. From him, for a trifling sum, they are acquired by a London bookseller who sells them to another bookseller, Bertram Dobell of Charing Cross Road; and he, honouring literature more than he covets cash, joins with William Brooke in a piece of literary detection which identifies the unknown genius as Thomas Traherne.

We now know that in 1637 the wife of a Hereford cobbler gave birth to a son, Thomas, who went up to Brasenose College, Oxford, and became a priest. Unlike the priest whom we shall meet at Hampton Court, Traherne had no worldly ambition. "I chose," he wrote, "rather to live upon 10 pounds a year . . . and feed upon bread and water, so that I might have all my time clearly to myself; than to keep many thousands per annums in an estate of life where my time would be devoured in care and labour." Traherne, in short, paid the price of his own artistry, which was poverty. He retired to his native Herefordshire, as rector of the parish of Credenhill. Fifteen years later he came to Teddington, as chaplain to Sir Orlando Bridgman, Lord Keeper of the Privy Seal; and there he died, aged thirty-eight, having written some memorable poems and the largest collection of mystical prose in our literature . . . things which seemed to have died with him, and indeed did die, until, like a phoenix, they arose from the dust of second-hand books.

Meantime, Trowlock Island appears, doing its best to distract attention from Kingston power station. Kingston is altogether a place to be passed, even although it does contain the King's Stone at which several Saxon monarchs were crowned. Here John

Galsworthy was born, in August 1867, at a villa called Parkfield on Kingston Hill; and here "Decline and Fall" Gibbon was schooled. Gibbon, in fact, became a child of the Thames; first at what he called "a day school at Putney" and afterwards "in my ninth year . . . I was sent to Kingston-upon-Thames, to a school of about seventy boys, which was kept by Dr. Woodhouse and his assistants". There, he remembered, "By the common methods of discipline, at the expense of many tears and some blood, I purchased the knowledge of the Latin syntax."

Presently a waterworks looms up, waging with Kingston power station a ding-dong battle for first place as the river's ugliest object. At such times it is advisable for the traveller to wear blinkers, finding what inward light he may from his own meditations—as, for example, on the name of this river, which it shares with several other English rivers, though they spell themselves differently: Tamar in Cornwall, Thame in Oxfordshire, Tavy in Devon. Caesar called it Tamesis. Tacitus called it Tamesa. Bede in 730 called it Tamisa. Other early variations were Temis, Temse, Temes. Ultimately the word comes from the Sanskrit *tamasa* (a tributary of the Ganges) meaning "dark river",—or, rather, the river with a muddy bed which causes its water to seem less "light" than water flowing over a pebbly bottom.

Having passed the waterworks, the Thames approaches the classic ground of Hampton Court, with Bushy Park and its deer on the right bank. Here another famous writer lived, in years when Teddington was a village. Unlike Traherne, R. D. Blackmore was famous during his lifetime, notably as the author of *Lorna Doone*, though that was only one of several of his fine novels. Richard Doddridge Blackmore was more than a bird of passage across the Thames. He was born on the river's upper reaches, and died on this reach. His mother died in 1825 when he was four months old. The father, who was Curate-in-charge at Longworth, then took the child into Devon, and gave him the classical west country education at Blundell's and Exeter College, Oxford. It was from the west country that Blackmore first gleaned the story of the Doones (chiefly from his grandfather, who had been vicar of Oare). Many years later Blackmore was teaching classics at a school in Twickenham, but the life did not suit him. To a friend he wrote: "Considering for some time what occupation to follow, I decided to become a gardener and horticulturist. Having studied botany and agricultural chemistry also, I felt that I was well-equipped for this calling." He therefore explored the Thames Valley "in search of suitable soil for pear cultivation for Covent Garden Market". He found what he wanted at Bushy Park—sixteen acres of fertile land within a dozen miles of Covent Garden. There he laid out his fruit farm, and designed a home for himself and his young wife. Gomer House he named it, after a favourite dog; and in it he spent the greater part of a long life, and wrote the best of his books. The house was demolished in 1938.

Now the river becomes wider, as though aware of an obligation toward Hampton Court, and then emphasizes its awareness by saluting with a slow and stately bend, accompanied by trees.

Hampton Court is a portrait in itself, and every traveller will wish to land alongside for a closer view. How shall one describe this palace that began as a rich man's retreat, became the home of kings and queens, and is now a national museum? Two aspects predominate: the silhouette and the colour. The silhouette is of roofs, gables, chimneys, towers; some high, some low; a type of hectic graph, full of meaning for eyes that can assess intrinsic harmony. And the colour? The colour is Time itself, woven into bricks that have mellowed from bright red to an indefinable haze of warmth: all this within a few yards of the river, and all conceived by a man who, before he had fully enjoyed it, bade farewell to his greatness.

Thomas Wolsey was born at Ipswich in 1472, reputedly the son of a butcher. In those years—the last of the medieval years—the Church welcomed any clever boy. Moreover scholarships abounded and were open only to talent. At the age of fifteen Wolsey graduated at Magdalen College, Oxford (whence his nickname of Boy Bachelor), was ordained priest, became Magdalen's bursar, and was soon afterwards sacked for spending its money without permission. Having taken a mistress, by whom he had a son and a daughter, Wolsey showed such skill in diplomacy that Henry VII employed him as an ambassador, and on Candlemas Day, 1509, appointed him Dean of Lichfield. Two months later the King died. This was a severe shock to the rising young diplomat, who now had to ingratiate himself with a new master, Henry VIII. From the very start the King's grandmother, distrusting Wolsey, used her influence against him; but patience and ability wore down all opposition. Within two years Wolsey was made a Privy Counsellor; while still in his forties he became Lord High Chancellor, Archbishop of York, Cardinal.

At the zenith of his power, the richest man in England, Wolsey built Hampton Court as his private palace, though he already owned magnificent houses at More in Shropshire and at Titten-hanger in Hertfordshire. His new palace contained "five fair courts" with rooms so many and so large "as to admit of two hundred and eighty beds, adorned with rich silk and gold hang-ings". Skelton summarized the Cardinal's eminence:

> Why come ye not to court?
> To whyche court?
> To the Kynge's Court,
> Or to Hampton Court?

Wolsey spent only a short time at his new palace, for soon after its completion, in 1520, he presented it to the King—not, as some people suppose, because he feared to seem greater than the King, but in order to emphasize that greatness by making a kingly gift. In fact, Henry did not take up residence at Hampton Court until 1525, and Wolsey himself sometimes stayed there after he had given it away. The extent of his retinue may be gauged by the quantity of food which it consumed at Hampton Court—four hundred and thirty oxen and nearly two thousand sheep in one year. Wolsey's retinue, indeed, outshone the King's. Whenever he went in state, he was preceded by two crosses, a Cardinal's and an Archbishop's. When he entered Parliament, even the benches were draped in scarlet to denote his presence. Soon, men said, he would become Pope and more powerful than the King of England. It was this pride which decreed Wolsey's downfall, more surely than his failure to secure the annulment of the King's marriage. The man who had set himself before his King—"*Ego et Rex meus*"—now appeared in the Court of that King's Bench, charged with tyranny, nepotism, incompetence, extravagance. Deprived of many of his honours, he patched a brief truce with Fate, but his ruin was irrevocable. Soon the King sent to arrest him.

Wolsey was then at Sheffield Park, south of Doncaster, a dying man. At Leicester, seeing that he could go no further, the monks received him into their abbey. To the last he denied that he had ever failed or crossed the King. To Sir William Kingston, who had come to take him to the Tower, he said: "If I had served my God so diligently as I have done the King, He would not have given me over in my grey hairs." He had foretold that he would die at eight o'clock next day; and, next day, as the clock struck eight, he died; so that his friends (as one of them wrote) "remembered his words of the day before, how he said that at eight of the clock we should lose our master".

They buried him obscurely at the abbey. All that he still possessed was forfeit to the King. When news of his death reached London, the citizens rejoiced; but there was one, a Court jester, who wept because the Cardinal had been kind to him.

Wolsey's palace of Hampton Court became the King's headquarters, which he enlarged and made even more magnificent. In its Great Hall James I saw the latest play by Shakespeare or Ben Jonson. From its wharf Charles I escaped to the Isle of Wight. Among its alcoves Charles II fondled his women. Queen Mary II and her Dutch husband commissioned Wren to demolish parts of Wolsey's design and to rebuild them after his own fashion. At Hampton Court Queen Anne confirmed Pope's couplet:

> Great Anna! whom three realms obey
> Dost sometimes counsel take—and sometimes tea.

Pope, by the way, set parts of his *Rape Of The Lock* in the palace.

The first two Hanoverian Kings completed Wren's unfinished additions, but George III would have nothing to do with the place; he had endured an unhappy childhood there. So, Hampton Court became a well-preserved husk, as it were a ghost haunting its own memories.

Too often a classic ground leads into an anti-climax. At Hampton Court this is not so. Scarcely three hundred yards ahead, on the right bank, the Mitre Hotel, draped in wisteria, looks as well as when it was built three centuries ago, as an unofficial annexe to the palace. Even Hampton Bridge—designed during the 1930s by Sir Edwin Lutyens—has enough red brickwork to blend with Wolsey's *pied-à-terre*.

A little above Hampton Bridge, at Molesey, the river wears its Sunday best throughout the week. Here the trees on the right bank excel themselves, and between them Molesey Lock announces an important feature of the portrait.

The purpose of a lock is plain; it is to facilitate the passage of boats from one level of water to another, which it does by creating a cistern that can be filled and emptied. Everyone who knows anything at all about Leonardo da Vinci is not in the least surprised to learn that it was he who invented locks (for the Mortescara Canal, which supplied Milan with water). The first English lock was built in 1563 (on the Exeter Canal, by a Welshman, John Trew) though from time immemorial the Thamesfolk had constructed timber dams to intercept fish and to increase the depth of water. Some of these dams had a crude sluice-gate, able to cause a flash (or flush) of water; thus the name flash-lock.

Throughout the middle ages and until relatively recent times these dams were a source of trouble. They did little to control floods, and much to aggravate them. Many millers used them in order to fleece the bargemasters whose craft had to pass through them. It was not until the eighteenth century that a system of effective locks was built. Most of the present locks were constructed during the nineteenth century by the Thames Conservancy Board. Until that Board was founded the Thamesfolk had lacked any one river authority to whom they might turn for help. Admittedly, the beginnings of a centralized supervision may be traced so far back as the year 1605, when parts of the upper river became unnavigable, and the Oxford and Burcot Commission was appointed to advise Parliament; but the Commission was soon disbanded, having built three locks.

More than a century passed before Parliament instituted the first overall authority, the Thames Commissioners, who, after prolonged ineffectiveness, built a series of locks between Maidenhead and Sonning. In 1774 the lock-keepers were given riverside sheds (which rotted away within a few years); in 1780 a towing-path was extended into Pangbourne; and in 1795 tolls were standardized, more locks constructed, the towing-path improved.

But these measures, which seemed to herald a new dawn, were really the harbingers of night, for the industrial revolution became a child of its own creations, and when railways began to wax, the river started to wane. By 1883 it had waned so steeply that the lock-keeper's wages were halved. The railways, it is true, brought new pleasure-craft to the Thames, but no amount of week-end traffic could redress the balance of lost commercial cargo.

In 1866 Parliament resolved that something must be done to halt and counteract the stagnation. Accordingly, the Thames

Commissioners, or Conservancy since 1857, were empowered to administer the river between Cricklade and Yantlet Creek in Kent. New locks were built, old tolls were modernized, sewage was diverted away from the river.

The Conservators took a realistic view of commercial traffic. They admitted that it was dwindling and would continue to dwindle. The Thames above Teddington had become chiefly a pleasure ground, and was to be preserved (in the words of the Thames Preservation Act) "for purposes of public recreation". In 1887 the Thames Conservancy Board refused to allow its buildings to display any form of advertisement; which is one reason why the locks are consistently handsome. Today the Conservators remain true conservatives, observing the maxim that when it is not necessary to change, it is necessary not to change: and when changes are necessary the Board ensures that they blend as closely as maybe with their background. In 1909 the supervision of the river below Teddington Lock was transferred from the Thames Conservancy Board to The Port of London Authority.

Beyond Molesey the river, which has been heading north towards the horrors of Hounslow, appears to get wind of that place, and at once changes course, making west for Sunbury. Having passed the new houses at Hurst Park race course—second by a short neck from Kingston power house in the race for ugliness—the Thames re-enters classic ground, for here stands the house to which Sir Christopher Wren retired at Hampton village, and near it the home of Sir Richard Steele, the essayist, which he named The Hovel. But even those great characters are overshadowed by David Garrick.

In 1753 Garrick rented a riverside house here, with garden, stables, and out-buildings. This he liked so well that he bought it, and set about converting it into a residence worthy of the foremost actor-manager of the day. Chippendale designed the furniture; new façades were devised by the Adams brothers (architects of Adelphi Terrace, whom Garrick called "Dear Adelphi"); and Capability Brown, that "marvellous boy" from Northumberland, was summoned from his work at Hampton Court, to lay-out a new garden. But Brown faced a dilemma because Garrick's Villa was separated from its garden by the turnpike road. Garrick wished to join them by a bridge; Brown recommended a tunnel; over, in fact, or under. The problem was solved when Garrick's old friend, Dr. Johnson, set his massive mind to it. "David, David," he cried, "what can't be overdone may be underdone." So, a tunnel was built, having three bathrooms supplied by a spring of pure water. It seems that England's leading actor was less widely known than one would have expected; at Hampton, some thirteen miles from London, the rating officer set him down in the books as David Garraik.

Garrick himself was the son of a Captain-Lieutenant of Dragoons. When therefore he did achieve greatness, the great found it easy to thrust themselves upon him. In 1755 Horace Walpole told a friend: "Today I dined at Garrick's. There were the Duke of Grafton, Lord and Lady Rochford, Lady Holdernesse, the Spanish minister." Garrick's Villa, in short, became a magnet, attracting many sorts of greatness. Hither came King Christian VII of Denmark, George Romney, the Duke of Devonshire, Hannah More, the Earl of Pembroke, Sir Joshua Reynolds, Queen Charlotte, Dean Stanley, and a host of Garrick's fellow-players, some of them to strut their hour of rehearsal. Neither before nor after was such splendour seen at Hampton. On 19th August, 1774, Mr. and Mrs. David Garrick celebrated their silver wedding (three months after that event) with "a splendid entertainment or Fête Champêtre at his gardens at Hampton" lit by 6,000 lamps, startled by innumerable fireworks (by courtesy of the Italian fireworker, Signor Torre, who had come, no doubt, at considerable pecuniary loss to himself, having cancelled a prior engagement at a place unspecified).

Long after Garrick's death ("it eclipsed the gaiety of nations", said Johnson) Mrs. Garrick resided at the Villa, where she was visited by George IV and Queen Charlotte. In 1820 Cruikshank made a sketch of her, "Aetat 97". To Dean Stanley she was "a little bowed old woman, who went about leaning on a gold-headed cane, dressed in deep widow's mourning, and always talking of her dear Davy".

But all that was to come. At Garrick's Villa today one's imagination recreates the prime of that place, the sound of a horse and carriage late at night, and the great man himself, still in his powder and paint, stepping down, pausing to savour the fresh air; and then, as though to shake off the lights and the audience, throwing himself full-length in the chair before a wintry fire; or, in summer, taking a nightcap turn beside the river: all peaceful, all silent, save when a chiming church reminds him that tomorrow night he must heighten that business with the Fool, or scribble a birth-day greeting for poor Peg Woffington.

Perhaps it was this riverside retreat which enabled Garrick to grow old like an oak, for when his retirement was at last an-nounced, Hannah More wrote: "He retires with all his blushing honours thick about him, his laurels green as in their early spring. Who shall supply his loss to the stage? Who shall now hold the master-key of the human heart? Who direct the passions with more than magic power?" One wonders what, if anything at all, Garrick would make of Comrades Beckett, Wesker, Brecht?

Beyond Garrick's Villa and the island named after him, the river endures a bad patch, crowned by a waterworks, and not perceptibly improved by Thornycroft's boat yards. On my last visit here I noticed a great deal of driftwood. This is not a new feature of the portrait, but it has become more conspicuous during the past twenty years; and in 1965 the Tideways' senior rowing club, London Rowing Club, formed a committee to propose remedies. Now, there is no authority that is compelled to remove debris from the river, but the Thames Conservancy Board is em-powered to do so, and has gallantly transformed a privilege into an obligation. During 1965 it collected thousands of tons of driftwood from the Thames below Teddington. Some of the logs were thirty feet long. Other unsolicited contributions in-cluded bicycles, perambulators, oil drums, bedsteads, and thirty yards of wire. In 1966 the Board launched two vessels specially designed to collect flotsam. It is unlikely that large logs will be encountered above Teddington Lock, but even at Windsor I have seen bedsteads floating down-stream.

To describe this reach of the river is extremely difficult because, more than any other above Teddington, it resembles the curate's egg. At one moment you might fancy yourself in deep country; at the next, even the trees flinch to see so many ugly houses. This rapid change of scene is especially evident at Sunbury, where several pleasant islands appear, and the river becomes suddenly very narrow above the tree-lined lock, but soon afterwards meets a rash of jerrydom which follows it for much of the way into Walton, where Caesar is said to have forded the Thames during his second invasion of Britain.

Presently the river turns north-west and then, like the kitten's

Hurley Lock

tail, grows dizzy among a series of curves at Shepperton, whose church, largely rebuilt in 1614, makes a pleasant picture, paving the way to better things. Green fields appear, and many small islands, one of them called D'Oyley Carte Island, after its operatic owner. Here, too, market gardens abound, as they did when Blackmore designed his own fruit farm at Teddington. The soil is almost as vivid as Devon's; not at all the typical London clay. People on the tops of omnibuses look down on sheep grazing an oasis in a prefabricated desert; and sometimes a landworker appears, seeming as out of place as Hardy's reddleman in a world of black bowlers and ebony jeans. At this point the river creates a maze of curves, and on the left bank, a little above Pharaoh's Island, Woburn Park takes its name from those curves—*woh* meaning "crooked", and *burna* meaning "a stream". Shepperton, also, offers a clue to the past of the portrait; the name comes from two old English words, *sceaphierda tun*, meaning "the settlement where shepherds live".

Having been joined by the River Wey, the Thames at Shepperton weaves among weeping willows and a number of bungalows, each with its trim craft and flower-filled garden. There was a ferry here, which recalls the most famous of all the Thames ferrymen, John Taylor, the Water Poet, who knew the river from Oxford to the Pool.

John Taylor was a Gloucester man, born in 1580 of poor parents who were nevertheless able to send him to a grammar school where, as he put it, having been "mired in Latin", he escaped from the mud by getting himself pressed into the Navy. "Seven times at sea," he boasted, "I served Eliza Queen." Thereafter he became a ferryman and a collector of dues payable on wine coming up-river. Even in those years the river traffic was feeling the pinch of overland competition ashore. "Hired hackney hellcarts" was Taylor's description of London cabmen.

In 1630 Taylor published a collection of verses. One stanza will show how bad they are, and how good:

> We went into a house of one John Pinner,
> And there eight several sorts of ale we had
> All able to make one stark drunk, or mad.

Anyone wishing to taste the Thames as it was during the reign of King Charles I may spend a profitable half-hour (not longer)

3

Medieval cloisters at Hurley

paddling through Taylor's collected works, which the Spenser Society of Manchester edited and published in eight volumes. But Taylor wrote prose also, and was quick to learn the value of gimmickry. Having announced that he would walk to Edinburgh without "borrowing, begging, or asking meat, drink or lodging", he did indeed walk to Edinburgh (and further yet, to Braemar) and did indeed publish an account of his journey, which he called *The Pennyles Pilgrim*; but was the journey so impecunious as he claimed? Before setting out, he had enrolled 1,600 prospective buyers of his book, some of whom afterwards refused to buy it, alleging that he had begged and borrowed throughout the journey.

On the Thames he organized another gimmick by sailing in a paper boat for thirty-six hours, supported by eight bladders, and propelled by two sticks tipped with dried fish. It was those exploits, rather than his poems, which explain why (in Southey's words): "Kings and Queens condescended to notice him, nobles and archbishops admitted him to their table, and mayors and corporations received him with civic honours."

Nor were his rewards solely of a sociable sort, for he was well-paid to devise Thames pageants for the Royal Family; notably a display to mark the marriage of the Princess Elizabeth and the Elector Palatine (and when Taylor's travel-journalism took him to the Princess's new home, she and the Elector invited the roving reporter to dine with them).

During the Plague Taylor rowed up-river to Oxford, where the Provost of Oriel—evidently not a literary man—granted him a room in college. During the Civil Wars Taylor remained loyal, and when the King set up his headquarters in Oxford, he made the ferryman a Yeoman of the Guard. Oxford, in fact, has one of Taylor's two portraits; the other hangs in the hall of the Watermen's Company in London.

All in all, this Water Poet was a man, or at any rate thick-skinned, for whereas Keats responded to malicious criticism by acquiring (or exacerbating) the tuberculi which killed him, Taylor responded by producing more verse, even although

> . . . some through ignorance, and some through spite,
> Have said that I can neither read nor write.

At Shepperton Ferry the towing-path crosses from the left to the right bank, and the river changes course again, from south-west to north-west, doubling back on itself as it leaves Chertsey Lock. The bridge at Chertsey is handsome and was built of Purbeck stone two centuries ago. The medieval Benedictine Abbey has gone, but its tithe-barn was restored to make an impressive monument. Chertsey's fourteenth-century bell sounds a curfew each evening from 29th September until 25th March. Thomas Love Peacock spent part of his boyhood at Chertsey, and Abraham Cowley the last two years of his old age. Cowley's house, in Guildford Street, has disappeared. It used to bear an inscription: "The Porch of this House, which projected ten Feet in to the Highway, was taken down in the year 1786, for Safety and Accommodation of the Public. Here, the last Accents flow'd from Cowley's Tongue," . . . not all of them being sweet, for having said (reasonably enough) "London is a monster," he proceeded to indict the entire Universe (in a letter to his friend Dr. Scarborough): "Life is an incurable disease."

From Chertsey to Laleham is a pleasant voyage, especially where the wooded grounds of Laleham House appear to the right, facing the green site of Chertsey Abbey, where monks fished on Friday. Laleham House—it is a convent now—was for many years the seat of the Earls of Lucan, one of whom witnessed the Charge of the Light Brigade, and will be introduced more formally in deeper country.

On the left bank, Laleham Ferry retains its charming Georgian cottage, and Laleham village still shows signs of its former identity. And this is true of many of the riverside places on this reach. Teddington, Shepperton, Hampton, Chertsey—each, in varying degree, offers a cluster of houses, or a *cul-de-sac*, that were built in the years before domestic architecture went out of fashion.

At Laleham we meet the ghost of yet another famous man, Matthew Arnold, who was born here in 1822, at the house where his father kept a small private school in the years before he became headmaster of Rugby. Neither the staff nor the pupils were Sybarites. Lessons began at 7 a.m. and continued until 3 p.m., with half-an-hour for breakfast. At 7 p.m. they were resumed until 9.30 p.m. Dr. Arnold himself taught for some fifty-four hours each week, beside writing massive works of scholarship and pedagogy, and begetting numerous children whom he nicknamed—Matthew Arnold, for instance, was Crab, and his brother

Tom became the Prawn. Matthew, indeed, received his first report when he was six months old, written by his father. It was
not encouraging: "Backward and rather bad-tempered." Although he mellowed with time, to become a scholar of Balliol
and a Fellow of Oriel, Matthew remained an indifferent naturalist,
claiming that he had heard blackbirds singing in December: the
author of *The Scholar Gipsy* ought to have recognized a missel-
thrush when he heard one. His birthplace was demolished, but
its site is marked by a cedar tree, in Ashford Road, which was
part of the Arnolds' garden. During the last fifteen years of his
life Matthew Arnold lived close to Laleham, in Pain's Cottage
at Cobham. The house was standing when I went there in 1964,
but seemed threatened by "development". Matthew Arnold was
buried in Laleham churchyard, beside several other members of
his family. It is customary to regard him as a typical Darwinian
doubter, but there were moments when emotion caused him to
set doubt aside, as in the epitaph to his father:

> Yes, in some far shining sphere,
> Conscious or not of the past,
> Still thou performest the word
> Of the spirit in which thou didst live.

From Laleham to Staines the Thames has rather too many
bungalows and Edwardian houses. Staines itself is a place to be
avoided. The river here is haunted by a vast cinema, uglier even
than the theatre at Stratford-on-Avon. A little above it is Staines
Bridge, built of granite by the son of John Rennie, the Hadding-
tonshire man who constructed the Kennet and Avon Canal (which
enters the Thames at Reading) and designed Waterloo, South-
wark, and London Bridges. Staines may have been named after
the *stane* or mile-stone on the Roman road nearby.

Above Staines Bridge a gigantic gas-container emphasizes that
most things bright and beautiful were not designed during the
twentieth century. Facing it, on the left bank, is the London
Stone, which marked the City's control of the Thames below that
point. "God preserve ye City of London" says an inscription, but
the stone itself is probably not the original boundary-mark; experts believe that its inscription was carved during the seventeenth
century.

Staines, like Kingston, is altogether a bad thing, yet it must not

be allowed to overshadow the fact that this reach of the Thames
is predominantly pleasant; the glaring blemishes are outnumbered
by the minor flaws, and the flaws by the miles of tree-lined fields
and gardens. Walking or boating, a traveller finds it difficult to
believe that he is hardly outside the Greater London area. There
are moments when he seems to be following a rural river whose
trees play hide-and-seek with a hinterland of park and meadow
and wooded hills. Nevertheless, it is this middling span—say,
from Charing Cross to Windsor—that has changed more drastically than the rest. Below Poplar the river retains its shipping;
above Maidenhead its ancient farmlands prosper and abound. But
the middle tract has lost both its ships and its shippons; and the
houses which it has acquired cannot be counted as gain. Some
relics of that other river—its water-mills, for example—have
appeared already; one at Chertsey, built by the monks; the other
just above London Stone, at a point where the River Colne
enters the Thames. But these features will be seen more memor-
ably up-river, when their story can be told in its proper setting.

The river meanwhile begins as it were to preen itself and to
discard its bungalows, as though aware that it has approached the
most classical of all its grounds: Runnymede, the scene of Magna
Carta.

At Runnymede the Thames rises to a royal occasion, for which
the country seems to have come to town, wearing a Sunday best.
On the left bank, meadows reach out towards hills topped by
many trees; on the right, the trees return that compliment by
coming down to the river, within sight of what is now a small
slice of America, marking England's tribute to President Kennedy.
Early in the morning, before the traffic has arrived, only the birds
are heard, and whatever sheep happen to be at hand.

The signing of Magna Carta ranks among the pre-eminently
important events that have taken place beside the River Thames.
Most people, indeed, regard the Great Charter as though it were
a Beveridge Plan, devised by "progressive" peers who had taken
to reading *The New Statesman*. That view is a caricature. Of all the
major English constitutional documents, few have done so much
to benefit the rich, and so little to relieve the poor. The bare facts
of the matter are as follows.

King John—an unlovely monarch, though less inept than the
textbook legend—has violated the laws of Edward the Confessor

as they were confirmed in a charter of King Henry I. A majority of the Barons, therefore, take up arms, to compel the King to honour that charter. Their action is not to be interpreted as un-alloyed public-spiritedness. Such spirits did exist among the nobility, but they were not numerous. To a great nobleman of the twelfth century the King of England was basically *primus inter pares*; so the Barons pit their privileges against the preroga-tive; and to King Henry's charter they add sixty-three clauses of their own. Some of these clauses concern chiefly the nobility—as, for example, the remarriage of the widows of tenants-in-chief; some concern chiefly the middle class of society—as, for example, the right of foreigners to trade with England; some, again, con-cern all classes—as, for example, the standardization of weights and measures. Religion, since it touches every aspect of the life of every medieval man, receives due attention. Indeed, the Great Charter begins by asserting the liberty of the English Church (a strange phrase in Catholic times, heralding an insular patriotism that is to become the ground of the Reformation).

Assuredly this Great Charter did much to protect the life, liberty, and property of all the King's subjects. But what does it signify today? Is it, as the average citizen believes—and as Hallam himself asserted—"the keystone of English liberty"? If it is, then so much the worse for English liberty. The Great Charter, for instance, insists that all law-abiding subjects be free to leave and to re-enter the kingdom as they wish. Today they are denied that right; they must buy a passport (and the State may withhold even that concession). The Great Charter insists that justice be done without payment. Today we must pay a lawyer (sometimes several lawyers), and even if we conduct our own case, we must still pay Court fees. The Great Charter (in its twentieth clause) insists that no fine be imposed if by paying it a man shall lose his "contentement"—that is, the ability to maintain himself and his family according to his station in life. Today anyone may be made bankrupt by damages awarded by just twelve men in a mood of immoral indignation (and the tax collector will sell everything a man has, from the Rolls-Royce to his collar stud). These facts may appear to be justified by present circumstances, but they make nonsense of anyone who cites Magna Carta as his constitu-tional *ipse dixit*.

And what of the famous signing of this Charter?

Point number one: the King of England did not set his Seal upon it solely because nobody had bothered to teach him how to write his own name. The King of England could write "John" as legibly as any man, and more clearly than some of his Barons. The Great Charter was confirmed by being stamped with seals, that being the custom of the day in matters of such high estate.

Point number two: at Runnymede is an inscription: "In these Meads on 15th June, 1215, King John at the instance of deputies from the whole community of the realm, granted the Great Charter, the earliest of constitutional documents, whereunder ancient and cherished customs were confirmed and abuses redressed, the administration of justice facilitated, new provisions formulated for the peace, and every individual perpetually secured in the free enjoyment of his life and property."

But there is at Runnymede another sign, pointing in another direction, towards an island named Magna Carta Island, where a Gothic cottage contains a stone, on which (they say) the Great Charter was sealed. I doubt it. They had tables, even in 1215. I doubt, too, the truth of the first part of the inscription on this stone, which says: "Be it remembered that on this island, in June, 1215, King John of England signed Magna Carta." It is true that Napoleon and the Czar did business in the middle of a river, but that was a face-saver, and in any event it took place on a raft. With the whole of England to choose from—and a large meadow nearby—it seems unlikely that the Barons really did go messing about in boats. At a time when knights wore heavy armour, a man overboard was a man overdue and very soon found to be missing. The inscription's second part I accept wholeheartedly. It says: "In the year 1834 this building was erected in commemoration of that great event by George Simon Harcourt, Esq., Lord of the Manor, and then High Sheriff of the County."

It is a pity that such contradictions should be publicized at Runnymede. The Charter itself states that the ceremony took place in a meadow—*in prato quod vocatur Runingmede*—"in a meadow called Runnymede". In 1921, by the way, the Commissioners of Woods and Forests tried to sell the meadow for as many pieces of silver as it would fetch. But somebody protested, and in 1929 Runnymede was acquired by The National Trust. What an opportunity was missed . . . King John's Snack Bar, Magna Carta Motors Limited, Barons' Incorporated Cement.

Whether in a meadow or on an island, the sealing of the Great Charter was a colourful event. Beside his personal retinue, the King was attended by the Archbishops of Canterbury and Dublin, the Bishops of Winchester, London, Lincoln, Bath, Worcester, Coventry. The Papal Legate was with them, and the Master of the Templars; also Alan, Lord of Galloway (one of the earliest Scotsmen to take the rich road southward) with the Earls of Arundel and Warren. The opposing company was even more dazzling, for it included (in the words of the chroniclers) "well nigh all the nobility of the English kingdom". Perhaps the most succinct account of the scene comes from Walter of Coventry: "At length, after much deliberation, they (the King and the Barons) made friends, the King granting them all that they asked and by his charter confirming this. The kiss of peace was exchanged, and homage and fidelity having been renewed, they ate and drank together, and the day for the completion of the pact was appointed." This "completion of the pact" refers to the final draft of the Charter, which was not ratified until the following Friday, 19th June. Before he went to meet the Barons, the King had probably received a preliminary draft, which he and his advisors used as the basis for discussion during the four days following. So it was that they set their mark upon an historic document, beside an historic river, in the presence of an historic company.

Having risen to an occasion, the river beyond Runnymede maintains that high tide, sweeping through woods and meadows, on towards Beaumont, the Roman Catholic school, which in 1965 agreed to merge with Stonyhurst, as an act of self-preservation. Behind Beaumont, Windsor Park makes it difficult to believe that the Thames has hardly passed beyond Greater London.

At Old Windsor Lock the Thames makes a horseshoe curve around Ham Common, but the New Cut drives due west towards Albert Bridge, leaving Old Windsor about a mile to the south. Both the river and the Cut are pleasantly wooded. Old Windsor has nothing much to offer nowadays, unless it be the grave of Mary Robinson, who in her time was better-known as Sappho (a poetess who produced a daily poem for *The Morning Post*) and as Perdita (an actress whom Garrick coached at his Villa in Hampton). He had hoped to present her as Cordelia, but she ran away to make a disastrous marriage. The Prince of Wales used her for a while, and then superannuated her at £500 a year. She died before her time, from a rheumatic complaint. Her portrait was painted by the *tres magi* of that art—Reynolds, Gainsborough, Romney.

Beyond Albert Bridge the Home Park of Windsor Castle presents arms with a regiment of handsome trees, rigid as sergeant-majors.

On the right bank stands Datchet, which even now retains traces of a seamanly past—its boats, its "beach", its white-topped boatmen. Datchet was the nest of a very rare bird indeed, an astronomeress, Caroline Herschel, sister to the great William, who, from his bachelor home in Bath, struck up a quasi-scientific friendship with George III. As a frequent visitor to Windsor Castle, William Herschel entertained the Royal Family with celestial soirées. "Last night," he reported to Caroline, "the King, the Queen, the Prince of Wales, the Princess Royal, Princess Sophia etc., saw my telescope." They also saw through it: "The King has very good eyes and enjoys observations with the telescope exceedingly." Herschel, in fact, received a royal pension, as well as two grants of money to buy equipment, and in the summer of 1772 he decided to live nearer to his royal patron. He therefore chose a house at Datchet—not, it seems, with a keen eye, for when Caroline arrived to supervise the furnishings, she found that the place had been empty for several years, and was surrounded by a rampart of weeds.

After two months of invasion by builders and decorators, brother and sister were able to resume their customary night watches; William calling out the data as he observed them; Caroline, with a clock and a candle, recording their precise time of arrival. At Datchet—and later from Observatory House in Slough—Herschel achieved lasting renown by discovering that the Milky Way possesses a Milky Way of its own, and is, as he expressed it, "an island universe". In 1924 Edwin Hubble of Mount Wilson confirmed the validity of Herschel's hypothesis; some of the luminary patches on the fringe of the Milky Way are outside the galaxy.

The Herschels' life at Datchet was not exempt from terrestrial trepidation. Thus, on 31st December, 1783, Caroline injured herself on a sharp hook attached to the telescope. When her brother shouted at her to hurry up: "I could only reply by a pitiful cry

'I am hooked'." The Thames Valley is damp, as Herschel discovered: ". . . not only my breath freezes upon the side of the tube of the telescope, but I more than once have found my feet frozen to the ground".

Caroline carved her own niche while she was at Datchet. Between 1786 and 1797 she discovered eight comets, and in 1783 she discovered three nebulae. Her diary for 2nd August, 1786, says: "Today I calculated 150 nebulae."

It is pleasant to record that, instead of ending sadly, like Charles and Mary Lamb, William and Caroline Herschel each in later life married and lived happily thereafter for so long that their combined ages made 180 years. When Caroline was eighty-three and living in Germany, she still enjoyed visiting a theatre. On her ninety-seventh birthday she entertained the Crown Prince and Princess of Prussia at her home, singing for them a song which her brother had composed half a century earlier. This remarkable old lady from Datchet died within sight of her ninety-eighth birthday, full of glory, wearing with easy grace a necklace of academic honours.

Datchet has, too, its music from another sphere, for it was at Datchet Mead that John and Robert, servants to a merry wife of Windsor, chucked Falstaff—"this gross watery pumpkin"—into "the muddy ditch close by the Thames side".

Ditton Park, on the outskirts of Datchet, was the seat of Sir Ralph Winwood, who unwittingly sent Sir Walter Raleigh to the scaffold. In 1616 Raleigh had already spent thirteen years in the Tower, a prisoner of the King's foreign policy, which sought to pacify both Rome and Spain; but the Overbury scandal, by breaking the pro-Spanish Earl of Somerset, enabled his anti-Spanish enemies to gain the King's ear. Among those enemies was Sir Ralph Winwood, a trusted ambassador. He urged James to release Raleigh so that he might go once more a'roving in search of riches and new lands, even although the venture would displease Spain, and perhaps singe some of its ships. Raleigh went, and failed, and returned, knowing that the penalty was death. He was arrested by one of his cousins, Sir Lewis Stukeley, Vice-Admiral of Devon, while travelling with his wife and a friend from Plymouth to London. The King refused a public trial, saying, "We think it not fit, because it would make him too popular. . . ."

Raleigh had written

> Give me my scallop-shell of quiet,
> My staff of faith to walk upon . . .

and his boon was granted. His last words were to the executioner, who had faltered: "What dost thou fear? Strike, man, strike." So was a great Englishman sacrificed to the policy of appeasing England's enemies. Sir Thomas Winwood did not live to see Raleigh's execution; he died while his friend was still at sea.

What, meanwhile, does the portrait begin to resemble? Has it begun to resemble anything at all? Or are its features simply a disjointed impressionism? I find it difficult to answer that question, even after many years' acquaintance with London's River. Perhaps the question never can be answered, away from the river itself. On the river, amid its sights and sounds, one inclines to believe that even here the Thames is more than the sum of its parts, and that it has, as we say, an atmosphere *sui generis* and immediately recognizable as such. If that is true, then it must be because history and architecture have combined to make it so; for there are no Thamesfolk hereabouts, and nothing that can be called a Thames countryside. And yet, after all, there may be one feature which, with the trees and the water, does transform still-life into a portrait: the fishermen. One saw them at Teddington, one would have seen them at Richmond, they will be seen at Lechlade.

Fishing on the Thames below Staines is open to the public, but above Staines it is not open to the public. In some parts, however (to cite the Thames Conservancy Board's admirably lucid instructions), "In some parts fishing is not objected to by the owners. In certain places the owners either do not allow fishing or require their permission to be first obtained whether fishing rights take place from the bank or boat. In one or two cases they may make a charge."

Night fishing is forbidden above Staines; below Staines it may not be done from a boat. The Authority will issue a yearly licence, to fish at twenty-two weirs between Old Windsor and Radcot. There is a closed season for coarse fish (from 15th March until 15th June) and another for trout (between 11th September and 31st March). From April until June trout-fishers must use rod and line with artificial fly, or spinning or live bait.

Fishing the Thames has played some part in our understanding of human physiology. In 1628 William Harvey published from Frankfurt an essay describing his discovery of the circulation of the blood; and to a scientific friend he wrote a postscript: "We have a small shrimp . . . which is taken in the Thames . . . the whole of whose body is transparent; this creature, placed in a little water, has frequently afforded myself and particular friends an opportunity of observing the motions of the heart with the greatest distinctness, the external parts of the body presenting no obstacle to our view, but the heart being perceived as though it had been seen through a window." Medical students will not find that shrimp above Teddington.

Anglers on the middle and upper Thames try for trout and tench, barbel and bream, grayling and gudgeon. Izaak Walton three hundred years ago reported that the Thames salmon were tastier than any others in the kingdom; and he ought to have known because he had fished the Dove and many another famous water. Even during the nineteenth century the Thames salmon were sometimes so plentiful as to glut Billingsgate Market, physically and metaphorically.

"Angling," wrote Izaak Walton, "is somewhat like poetry; men are born to be so." Certainly the Thames attracts such men —and such women and children also. From dawn till dusk, in every kind of weather, they wait like Rodin's pensive statue, hoping (with Mr. Micawber) that something will turn up. Of them I shall say only this, that from their fishing they land the sort of peace which passes my own understanding; and who shall deny that the loss may not be mine?

Meantime Romney Lock offers a preview of Sylvan Suburbia, with its trim garden, white stakes, and tree-lined towing path; all creating an idyll, and all so near to London.

So the Thames proceeds, from due west to south-east. Away to the right, Buckinghamshire's only industrial town—the vast Slough of despond—is hidden by trees and fields. One sees instead the playing-fields of Eton and the roof of the College chapel.

Thereafter the water became so foul that the fish died, but during the 1960s a cleaning-up enabled most of the fish to return.

IV

SYLVAN SUBURBIA: WINDSOR TO COOKHAM

THE castle glides into view dramatically and under false colours, because those medieval walls are not medieval; they were built during the nineteenth century. Even so, Windsor Castle is the most impressive of all the royal homes. As Celia Fiennes remarked of another building: "It looks finely."

William the Conqueror chose the site a thousand years ago, and on its artificial mound he raised a fortress. The guidebooks are mistaken when they describe William's castle as a royal residence. Neither he nor his successor lived in it. Their palace was at Old Windsor, below Albert Bridge. It was King Henry I who converted the castle into a palace, but of his work, as of the Conqueror's, nothing remains. Extensive building took place between 1350 and 1373, with William of Wykeham as Clerk of the Works from 1356 until 1361.

Henry III added to the walls, and built three towers. Edward III demolished much of the castle, and raised the Round Tower (which is less circular than its name suggests). Three Kings built Saint George's Chapel—Edward VI, Henry VII, Henry VIII. Queen Elizabeth added the north terrace and a gallery overlooking it. The State Apartments were renovated by Charles II. New buildings were commissioned by George IV, who chose Jeffrey Wyatt as his architect.

Wyatt was something of a card. Having secured the commission, he changed his name, partly in order to avoid being mistaken for his uncle (who also was an architect, and a better one) but chiefly in order to add an orotund echo to the knighthood which his services were expected to receive. Tradition says, when Wyatt sought royal permission to add *ville* to his name, the King replied: "Veal or mutton—call yourself what you like." It would be misleading to say that Sir Jeffrey Wyatville rebuilt Windsor

Castle, but between 1824 and 1840 he did make many interior changes, and designed most of what is visible from the river.

Unlike the Tower of London, or the palace of Whitehall, Windsor Castle was a place where the Sovereign relaxed. Even today one thinks of it in terms of polo and informal royal occasions. To that extent, therefore, the Castle's warlike appearance is deceptive; yet how impressively the towers and ramparts dominate the river. Windsor, however, has several other notable features . . . for example, its two railway stations, evocatively Victorian. Almost you can smell the maccassor and the lavender; almost see the punts, the pugs, the parasols; almost hear the household names . . . Gladstone, Crimea, Ladysmith, Mr. Kipling, and (*sotto voce*) Lily Langtry.

Windsor's Theatre Royal flourished before Irving was born. Today, it is among the leading repertory companies. Like several of the local shops, it enjoys royal patronage.

A less exalted feature of Windsor was the coal stores, into which Bishop Bonner cast several Protestants during the reign of Mary Tudor. But the Protestants were not the first occupants of this Black Hole of Windsor, for in 1465 a certain John Payn was ordered, for political reasons, to lay false charges against his master: "And because that I would not," he complained to the Paston family, "they would have sent me to the coal-house at Windsor".

Windsor town hall was completed by Sir Christopher Wren, from a design by Sir Thomas Fits, who died while the work was in progress. The burgesses, mistrusting Wren's expertise, ordered him to reinforce the roof of the council chambers with extra pillars. Wren obeyed, but confirmed his handiwork (and confounded his critics) by making the columns support nothing except their own weight. They do not quite reach the ceiling which they were supposed to support.

Wren's father was Dean of Windsor, and the son became one of the town's two members of Parliament (the pair being halved in 1867). One must feel glad that Wren's plan to rebuild Windsor Castle was never executed, for his reconstruction of Hampton Court suggests that he would have transformed the castle into a palladian palace, with a medieval fortress tacked on. His home, by the way, is now a hotel near the bridge. "This house," says a tablet, "was built and occupied by Sir Christopher Wren 1676."

One assumes that the claim is valid, though I can find no other record of Wren's residence there.

There is, however, ample record that Milton lived near Windsor, on the site of what is now a large house called Berkyn Manor, in what used to be the village of Horton. Milton's father retired to Horton in 1632, and Milton's mother was buried in the church. Milton himself spent six years at Horton, where he composed *L'Allegro, Il Penseroso, Lycidas, Comus* and *Arcades* (whose lyrics were inspired by Henry Lawes).

Two miles north of Windsor, in what has become the abominable desolation of Slough, Dickens lived awhile with his mistress, an actress named Ellen Ternan. That was in 1867, at a cottage in High Street. Twenty-two years later the cottage was demolished. Today the site contains a shop. Five years after Dickens's death, the mistress married a clergyman, Reverend George Robinson, who became headmaster of a school at Margate. Mrs. Robinson did not die until 1914.

Windsor itself is a cross-section of Time; always at heart genteel; for more than a century a riverside haunt; and now, with its milk bars and cinema, a garden for industrial Slough.

Eton, which stands on the right bank, is older than Windsor. Its name—*eyot-tun*—or "island fortress"—remains appropriate, for Eton still is a bastion: "the finest school", Defoe held, "that is in Britain, or, perhaps, in Europe".

It was on 5th July, 1441 that King Henry VI laid the foundation stone of Eton College Chapel. Its first headmaster was a Wykhamist, William Waynflete, who soon afterwards became Provost. In September of the previous year the King had issued the foundation charter, decreeing that the College should consist of a Provost, ten Fellows, four Clerks, six choristers, a schoolmaster, twenty-five poor scholars, and a similar ration of infirm old men. Free instruction in grammar was to be given to an indefinite number of poor boys from any part of the world. Twenty of the original pupils were of the nobility and gentry, and lived in College; other boys were allowed to dine in hall. As all the world knows, the noblemen and the gentlemen ultimately took possession of the place, though never to the exclusion of its poor scholars. Today the Eton boys adorn their narrow High Street, hatless with coattails swaying; pausing awhile before the sort of book shop, bun shop, and shirt shop that is to be found in Bond Street, Oxford, and Cambridge, but scarcely anywhere else in the world. In 1966 it was announced that the College uniform might be changed, so that Eton boys could look less like themselves and more like other people. A few days later the Provost announced that no such change would occur; so, for the time being, a plainly penny world will continue to be enlivened by tuppenceworth of colour. But Eton itself is something more than an ornament, for if the greater ever can encompass the lesser, then it does so at a modern public school, where service is taught as a mode of self-expression, with an insistency not to be found in other nurseries. At Eton, in its buildings and traditions, are to be seen those outward and visible signs that must surely inspire whatever of inward and spiritual grace resides among small boys and imaginative youths. The flower of Eton is perennial and sweet, and it flourishes despite a crop of ornamental weeds. How else shall we explain the devotion which it bred in such an austerely sensitive spirit as Robert Bridges, who, as an elderly man, could recapture the impact of Eton on a child:

> Here is eternal spring; for you
> The very stars of heaven are new;
> And aged Fame again is born
> Fresh as the peeping flowers at morn.

The College, the Castle, the River: if I were asked to name the sector of the Thames which most vividly distils the essence of what the word "stately" was intended to convey, I would choose this sector, even before others less urban; for here the Thames sweeps through a lordly arc; upon the one side, royalty; upon the other, noblesse; each still breathing beneath the swaddling clothes of modern life.

London River, I suggested, is evoked by the celestial seaway of Holst's Jupiter suite. The river at Windsor recalls Elgar. From his music, its blend of martial and mystical, the Thames leaps alive—serene, majestic, saddened inexpressibly by what the centuries have taught, yet never sullied, never cynical, never modish. No other notes than Elgar's so well enshrine the history, the humour, the heartache.

Suddenly, as the Castle falls astern, you are amazed because, suddenly, you are afloat in open country. To the right, after one sharp bend, the meadows reach for an apparently unpeopled

River steamer bound for Hambleden

horizon. What has happened, you ask, to these acres of valuable factory sites; these rods, poles, and perches of cloud-capped pent houses; these cubic feet of serve-yourself? The answer, the amazing answer, is—they are not for sale.

On the left bank the pleasant Alexandra Gardens invite the promenade which they create. Athens is there—the Eton boy's bathing place—and the enclosed Cuckoo Weir, where the junior boys swim. These are followed by a number of amiable chalets, their trim lawns trickling to the water. Further still, a rash of caravans seeps alongside, as though to emphasize that it is both useless and unjust to blame the Thames River Authority for this sort of outrage. The fault lies with individuals who are unfit to practise *laissez-faire* and with officials who are afraid to impose State control. The Authority—to make the point again—deserve praise for every riverside building which bears their imprint, and for their efforts to conserve whatever of beauty is compatible with necessity.

Presently Boveney Lock creates a sylvan scene—there is much lilac here—and from it the Castle astern resembles an indigenous cloud, windproof and rooted. Boveney church, clustered among trees, is a small Norman building, with timber tower and walls three feet thick. Here indeed the river grows green—"verdant" is the proper name for it—and never before have the trees stood so thickly to attention.

Now comes an acute bend to starboard, and, on the port bow, Oakley Court, so towered and turreted and twiddled that it achieves a caricature of itself. This is a Victorian notion of the good life. I cannot tell you who used to live here, nor who still does live here, because I have never felt even the slightest urge to inquire. In any event, the former are certainly dead, and the latter, if they are wise, have decided to move. Oakley Court, with its bric-a-brackery of arrow-proof attics, leads one to ask why it was the Victorian era, so rich in literature, was in all the other arts so poor that it may fairly be accounted bankrupt, except for a few men whose best works were done when the era was either dead or dying. It is a remarkable fact, that Morris, Pater, Ruskin—the wise men of fine arts—cherished many nick-nacks which to us seem clumsy, pretentious, pernickety.

Down Place, by contrast, which soon follows, is neat, well-bred, free of fiddleybits. It used to be the home of Jacob Tonson, who

4

Springtime at Fawley

discovered that to sell books is more profitable than to write them. Here he entertained the Whig wits—Walpole, Addison, Congreve—and here they founded the famous Kit-Kat Club, so called (it is said) because of the meat pies that were supplied by a Thames baker named Kit Catt. Tonson himself became the club's first secretary. In theory it was a literary club; in practice it plotted to build the House of Hanover on the site of the Stuarts.

Now Monkey Island appears, and on it a Victorian house containing part of an eighteenth-century fishing lodge of the third Duke of Marlborough. The ceiling of that older part is adorned with paintings of monkeys wearing eighteenth-century costume, so that one supposes the island to have been named after them. Some antiquaries, however, attribute the name to the monks who once owned the land. I cannot see that it matters. The point is, Monkey Island looks well. It persuades us—whom the rest of the world regards as islanders—to think how romantic it would be to live on an island.

Above Monkey Island the river enters the zenith of sylvan suburbia, overhung with willows, among them just enough gardens to seem companionable. This is the answer to all who would slight the suburban Thames, or skim it hurriedly in search of open country.

Presently the willows on the left give way, discovering some Edwardian pleasure houses, each garden striving to seem more flamboyant than the rest. Even in October their lawns are as baize as a butler's apron. When these houses were built, they stood in undoubted countryside. They still do retain the air of Galsworthyland, with a bowler hat and striped trousers ready for Monday morning. This is Frederick Lonsdale's notion of rural England. Yet it is pleasant. It is, in the proper sense, picturesque. The lady of Rupert Brooke's poem would have been right to call it "pretty". And through the prettiness the river glides, on towards Bray.

Bray has been old, and now is young; it was simple, and became sophisticated. Its Tudor cottages wither in suburban soil. Like artficial flowers, they are decorously dead.

If you land at Bray—and I cannot consider a landing worthwhile, because Bray is simply an urban imitation of rural originals which abound up-river—but if you do land, you will never find Bray's fickle vicar, who declared:

That whatsoever King shall reign,
I'll still be the vicar of Bray, Sir.

Even the man's name is elusive. Thomas Fuller said he was a Tudor
incumbent, Simon Aleyn, twice a Roman Catholic, twice an
Anglican; but Bray church has a memorial to another trimmer,
Francis Carswell, who several times turned his own clerical cloth
between 1667 and 1709.

Bray, at all events, is the first place *en route* which resembles a
village, and since the river will soon enter a realm of villages,
this would seem to be the moment for brief self-examination. As
one who detests towns, and never enters them except, like Falstaff, on compulsion, I have continually to remind myself that
these havens of thatched eaves, stately mansions, and fore-locked
folk were not a paradise. They stood upon purgatory, and no
man alive today would choose to live in them. The human suffering would appal him. The stench would sicken him. Three centuries ago men chained the insane, burned the heretic, grovelled
to the rich, chased a starveling into the next parish. Two centuries
ago a mother of twelve children was surprised if six of them survived infancy, and astounded if she herself lived to be sixty. Even
a century ago little children toiled ten hours a day in the pits;
surgeons, sawing without anaesthetics, prided themselves on their
blood-stained aprons; after a bad harvest not a few villagers
starved on berries and cats and dogs. To be sure, they enjoyed
many boons which we lack. They relished quietness. They moved
leisurely. They engaged in conversation among themselves, and
did not sit gnawing their fingernails because the death of a great
man had postponed the television jazz contest. And these facts
also must be remembered, for unless they are remembered, and
balanced against those others, the average visitor to an English
village will see little except the paper roses of his own spectacles.

After Bray the river endures an unpleasant quarter-of-an-hour
while it makes its way towards Maidenhead.

The name Maidenhead comes from the Middle English,
Maydenhythe, which means "The maidens' landing place". I do
not know what good (or bad) bait tempted medieval maidens to
disembark at this place. No bait at all would lure me from the
river's comparative safety. Maidenhead nowadays is ugly, shape-
less, noisy; and whatever slight interest it does possess should be

read about, from a distance, as follows: the handsome road bridge
was built in 1772 by Sir Robert Taylor who, like his contemporary, Dr. Bentley of Trinity, was the son of a stonemason. Taylor
did not begin to practise architecture until he was forty. Thereafter he designed the Bank of England and parts of Lincoln's Inn.
Having achieved a fortune as well as a knighthood, he bequeathed
£180,000 to the University of Oxford, for the building of the
Taylorian Institute, the headquarters of modern linguists.

Near Taylor's bridge are two almshouses; one of them ancient,
the other modern. The ancient were built in 1659 by a sailor
called Smyth. The modern were built by a businessman named
Herring, who, like Taylor, was born a pauper, died a rich man,
and gave much to charity.

In Saint Ives road you can see the house that was occupied by
Anne of Cleeves, one of King Henry VIII's more fortunate wives
(her marriage lasted a mere six months, unlike her life, which
continued for another seventeen years, and was crowned by a
royal pension and a tomb in Westminster Abbey).

Neither of Maidenhead's two churches is notable, but at the
railway bridge the imagination finds food for thoughts that will
sustain the brief voyage through ugliness. This bridge—it is the
finest of its kind on the Thames—has the world's widest brick
span (128 feet) and a truly resounding echo, as anyone will
discover if, when passing beneath it, he cares to call his own name.
At this bridge one remembers the man who might have claimed
to be the first professional explorer of the river: Isambard Brunel.

Isambard Kingdom Brunel was born at Portsea, in 1806, the
only son of a Norman emigré. Both father and son were knighted
for services to civil engineering. It was on 21st February, 1833
that Brunel first scribbled in his diary a cryptic BR, or Bristol
Railway, which was to become the Great Western. Brunel's task
was simple, and dauntingly difficult. Having studied a map of the
Thames Valley, he went out and walked across it, rode across it,
took coaches across it, explored it from boats, gazed down upon
it from hills, peered up at it from marshes. To read his diary is to
recapture the pioneering spirit which so changed the portrait of
the Thames that parts of it became unrecognizable, even while he
lived. On one September morning Brunel "started at 6 a.m.,
examined the ground in the neighbourhood of Wantage . . .
breakfasted at Streatley . . . returned to Reading, dined, and went

to Theal". A few days later he was "Up at 5 a.m. . . . ranged on the island east of Caversham. Breakfasted and mounted. Rode to meet Hughes; found him in barley west of cottage. Rode to Basildon Farm . . . rode on to Streatley; tried in every way to find a line round instead of crossing the river at Goring; found it impossible."

Walking or riding, early and late, through every change of climate, Brunel surveyed the country of the Thames; sometimes wading waist-high through corn-fields that were soon to bear a railway. At remote inns he would pore over his maps until dawn had snuffed the candles, and it was time to saddle-up and ride through the stubble or the mud. "Between ourselves," he confided to a friend, "it is harder work than I like. I am rarely at it much under twenty hours a day." He was then twenty-seven years of age.

The river passes under two more of his bridges, at Moulsford and at Basildon, and each combines beauty with usefulness; but Maidenhead Bridge is the finest of its kind on the Thames, and was built so well that it withstood the alarm that was sounded at two o'clock of a wild Sunday morning in November, when Brunel received word "that the Maidenhead Bridge was reported in a dangerous state and that the 6 o'clock train must not go over it". Like Wren among the burgesses at Windsor, Brunel had faith in his own handiwork, which Time continues to justify. When the traffic between Taplow and Didcot was quadrupled during the 1890s, engineers decided that there was no need to change the fabric of Maidenhead Bridge, and when the time came for them to build extra arches, they copied Brunel's.

Nor were bridges his only contribution to the portrait. He designed many of the Thames Valley stations—even their signals and shunting equipment. At Maidenhead and Slough, in Windsor and Goring, he created a railwayscape unmistakably Great Western. Trollope claimed that foxhunting was an excellent way of getting to know Essex; it landed him in so many ditches. Brunel might have claimed that engineering was an excellent way of getting to know the Thames; it led him through so many unbeaten tracks.

Our own track, meanwhile, leaves Maidenhead behind, and with it a number of those stridencies which Bishop Creighton arraigned when he said: "Vulgarity is an inadequate conception of the art of living." There are riverside places uglier than Maidenhead, but none so glossy.

After Maidenhead the Thames begins a long and straight course north-west, past Boulter's Lock, which has become hackneyed. In an era of punts and parasols the lock may have been handsome. Today it is the river's Piccadilly. Beyond it the Thames becomes suddenly so narrow that two steamers must pass each other warily. This is perhaps the most intimate vista so far, lined by trees standing thick as policemen on a royal occasion, as if to prepare us for a shock, because "shock" is the likeliest word with which to describe the initial response of a sensitive person on first seeing Cliveden Reach . . . shock at the height (the unexpected height) of the hills that sheer away from the right bank, at the luxuriance of their many trees, at the path which burrows among those trees, to become in summer a dappled avenue, and in autumn a brown study. And as though to heighten the steepness, the meadows on the left bank are level. Whether this is indeed countryside is a matter of taste, but that it appears to be countryside is a matter of fact. London at this point grows abruptly faint. Even the charm of Monkey Island seems formal and urban.

Cliveden Reach—they pronounce it Cleevedon—is one of several which may claim to be the most beautiful on the Thames. As you glide along, under the precipice of wooded hills, you notice what looks to be a small white chalet, high on the starboard bow; and you wonder how many beeches they needed to fell, before they could build such a place: but when it draws nearer, the small chalet becomes a mansion. The first great house here was built by Steenie's heir, the second Duke of Buckingham. It was enlarged by the Earl of Orkney, and rented by the Prince of Wales, father to King George III, who there saw the first public performance of Thomson's new masque, *Alfred*. The music for this masque was composed by Dr. Arne, and among the songs was one that we now call *Rule, Britannia*. Although I am not among those who rejoice in the fact, it is nevertheless true that the theme of Thomson's song has fallen forever behind the times, and ought no longer to be regarded as an unofficial national anthem. Since the first stanza of the song is persistently misquoted, even at Promenade Concerts, some people will care to know what it was that Thomson wrote:

When Britain first, at Heaven's command,
Arose from out the azure main,
This was the charter of the land,
And guardian angels sung this strain—
'Rule Britannia, rule the waves;
Britons never will be slaves.'

The house which first heard that song was destroyed by fire in
1795, and remained ruinous until Sir George Warrender bought
it in 1830. After a second fire, and two more ducal owners, the
present Cliveden Court was designed by Sir Charles Barry (architect of the House of Commons) with additions by the American
Astors. In 1942 Lord Astor gave most of the estate to the National
Trust, but retained his right to reside at the Court.

Here, on 16th January, 1667, was fought an infamous duel; not
between two men, but among six: on the one side, the Duke of
Buckingham, Sir Robert Holmes, Captain William Jenkins; on
the other, the Earl of Shrewsbury, Sir John Talbot, Bernard
Howard (a grandson of the Earl of Arundel). Each man was
wounded, and one was killed: all because Shrewsbury's wife was
Buckingham's mistress. The woman herself was a typical piece
of trash; and there are reasons for believing that she chose to
watch the duel, disguised as her lover's page. The duel need never
have been fought, for the King, having got wind of it, ordered
the Duke of Albemarle to arrest Buckingham, or by some other
means prevent the fight. In the event, both the King and Albemarle assumed that the other had taken steps to halt the matter,
so six men fought despite a royal veto. Pepys described the
scandal, on the day following: "The whole house full of nothing
but the talk of this business; and it is said that my Lord Shrewsbury's case is to be feared, that he may die." He did die, two
months later, of his wounds.

Even so, Cliveden Court is simply an ornament, fashioned to
the tastes of an ornamental age. The beauty of the Thames at
Cliveden would abide were the Court to be razed for a third time.
This memorable reach ought to be seen at six o'clock of a summer's morning; or at noon in October when the mist has retreated, and the trees are on fire; or at night (for night is a part
of the portrait, as valid as day and more mysterious). "I have been
one acquainted with the night" wrote Robert Frost; and night
itself can reveal old acquaintance in the guise of a stranger. Here,

while looking down at your feet, you may steer by the stars above your head. Sometimes the nightingales sing among the woods, mingling with the moon, as Verlaine foretold: ". . . *leur chanson se mêle au clair de lune*". Through long watches of a summer night the silence seems absolute. Towards dawn it may become absolute, except when a fish gobbles up, broadcasting the news with waves that carry it ashore. While you scull, slowly through fan-shaped moonlight, you find that you are striving to seem noiseless, as though walking in a cathedral at servicetime. You pause, counting the diamond-drops that quiver on the blade before they fall. Somewhere far away two young people, immersed in making their own memories, crackle a sports car through receding silence. A lark leaps up, half a mile off, spiralling its song towards the stars; and unless you happen to know about larks, you will glance at your watch (thinking it may have stopped) or towards the east (seeking the dawn). You may even observe that a rabbit on the bank has been observing you. Once in a life-time—probably not more than once—you will hear what seems to be the creaking of a woman's stays; and looking up, you will see an echelon of swans, like aircraft eluding the searchlight. If they come down upon the water nearby, you will marvel at their sudden transformation from wild geese into white ornaments. I once had a curious experience at Cliveden, which I afterwards recorded:

> I could have sworn that it was snow,
> So white the river seemed
> With icicles arrayed to glow
> Like blades of glass that gleamed.
> But I was wrong, and she was right
> —the Moon, that from her prime
> Descanted on the summer night
> Inaudibly, with rime.

These things are revealed only to the man who, having gone out to meet the river, sits down before it, and waits while it comes towards him.

When at last the Cliveden woods fall astern, it seems that all thereafter must become an anti-climax; but it is not so. Having taken away our breath, the Thames withholds it until we gasp; for the woods receding astern are replaced by others rising ahead. Nearby is the gracious-sounding My Lady Ferry, marked by a cottage on the Buckinghamshire bank, composed chiefly of fairy-like gables. Here the towing path comes into the open before plunging back among overhanging trees. Presently Formosa slides into view, the river's largest island, some fifty acres of grass and woodland concealing the remains of an eighteenth-century pleasure house. A few hundred yards more, and the river, though still girded by woods, narrows abruptly as it enters the first lock which can truly be called rural.

Cookham Lock is not my own favourite—that waits far ahead —but most people will agree that, of all the Thames locks, it was the most magically sited. It is woods, woods, woods all the way; fore and aft, to starboard and port, so that in April the birds from either bank create a singing gallery, and in October the trees create a Lucretian *flammantia moenia mundi*, "the flaming ramparts of the world".

Cookham village will please everyone who admires a pretty picture. Its red-brick cottages glister with white paint, and the ford and the village green makebelieve that they are not in commuterdom. The church has been spoiled inside, but its timber porch prevails. There is a memorial to a Thames artist, Frederick Walker, who, in a short life of thirty-five years, did some good work. In or about 1858 Walker apprenticed himself to the engraver Whimper. Afterwards, as an illustrator for *The Cornhill Magazine*, he came to know Thackeray, and was employed to illustrate some of his tales. Walker's best paintings are of Bray Ferry and Bray Almshouses. Here, too, lived a twentieth-century artist, Stanley Spencer.

Cookham Bridge (1867) remained a private toll bridge until 1947. From it there is an idyllic backward glance, with the river trisecting itself among backwaters; one of which, Odney backwater, is a favourite berth for boaters. Among the white boathouses on the right bank stands the office of the man who looks after the royal swans, which are a feature of the portrait.

Every year, in August or late July, the Thames swans are upped, which is to say counted, classified, and (some of them) marked. This ancient ceremony leads the imagination backwards through many centuries and among bizarre byeways. Some experts have stated, though none has proved, when the first swans reached England. The 1843 edition of *British Birds* claimed that King Richard I imported them from Cyprus; but why from Cyprus, when the birds were to be found nearer home, in Denmark? It is possible that the swans arrived uninvited, if only because they were able to do so. In 1771, for example, a swan that had been shot on the Thames carried a golden device which proved that it belonged to the King of Denmark; and a century later one of Queen Victoria's swans flew from the Thames to Stettin in Germany, where it was identified.

During the middle ages the swan became so much a table delicacy that Henry III and his guests consumed forty birds for their Christmas dinner at Winchester. Swans were royal birds (although, unlike the three fishes royal, they were never formally regalized by Act of Parliament). The Crown claimed all swans found at liberty on common water. Rarely was a subject allowed to take such swans. Among the subjects so honoured were the Warden and College of the King's Free Chapel at Windsor, who for seven years were permitted to take unmarked swans from the Thames between Oxford and London Bridge.

Towards the end of the sixteenth century, Swan Motes, under letters patent, empowered a commissioner to summon and swear juries to try all offenders against the swan laws. The earliest record of a Thames Swan Mote was made in 1566, when a number of the gentry were instructed "to enquire of such offences as have ben and are committed against thauncient lawes and Orders made for the preservation of the Queen's . . . game and herd of Swanns within the countie of Buck".

Soon after that time the feudal restrictions were relaxed, and it became fashionable to keep swans on private water. The marking of swans created a kind of heraldry; some owners borrowed of their coat of arms; the non-armigerous devised a code of noughts and crosses. In 1541 the Thames swans belonging to John Hastings of Oxfordshire were blazoned as *"Or, a maunche gules."* An obscure owner named Smartfoot marked his swans with crosses and rectangles.

The present Keeper of the Queen's Swans holds one of the most venerable offices in the kingdom; how venerable is not precisely known, but the office probably existed as early as the thirteenth century. Its full style was Master of the King's Game of Swans; shorter versions were Master of the Game, Swan-Master, Royal Swanherd, Chief Swannerd. The Swanherd is usually known as the Keeper.

During the sixteenth century, when the keeping of swans became fashionable as well as less restricted, the keepership acquired a new prestige. In 1553, for instance, it was held by Sir William Cecil of Burghley; in 1593 Lord Buckhurst became Master of the Swans for the whole of England; and in 1682 the office was held by the Earl of Manchester. Thereafter fashion followed its own custom and became *démodé*. By 1799 the Master of the Swans was plain "Dick Roberts". Unlike his illustrious predecessors, Roberts did not hold a sinecure. He was paid for doing a job himself.

Most of the Thames swans belong to the Crown; the rest are owned by two City guilds, the Vintners and Dyers, which acquired that right during the late fifteenth century. For several generations the Keepership of the Royal Swans has been held by members of the Turk family at Cookham. Another member of that family was Swan Master to the Vintners' Company in 1966; in which year the Dyers' Swan Keeper was Mr. H. C. Cobb of Putney.

Swan-upping on the Thames is a colourful pageant. Officials in six boats, representing the Crown and the two guilds, row in state from the Pool of London to Henley-on-Thames, wearing a vivid costume (it varies slightly among the three interests) of woollen caps, white trousers, and striped jerseys; with blazers for the men who mark the birds. Since 1910 the Royal Swans have been exempt from marking. All other mature swans—"clear-bills" as they are termed—receive one or two nicks on their side or mandible, according as they belong to the Dyers or to the Vintners. By order of Her Majesty Queen Elizabeth II the Thames swans are maintained at some 600 birds, of which about 500 are royal.

English swans are commonly known as mute swans, but they will hiss loudly enough should anyone attack them or their cygnets. During the breeding season the cob, or male bird, has a black marking on its bill. Whether these swans are dumb or not, the Greeks held that even the mutest of them will sing sweetly when death bids it so. Socrates, on the point of death, still cared well enough for truth to deny that a swan-song is sad. "Swans," he declared, "are prophetic birds because they know what happiness they will have in the next world."

These stately features of the portrait may be seen far down-river, soliciting tit-bits from the galley of an ocean-going steamer; and their country cousins may be seen far up-stream, confirming Andrew Young's simile:

> How lovely are these swans,
> That float like high proud galleons.

At Cookham the Thames offers an example of its own notion of progress. Thus, from Boulter's Lock overland to Great Marlow is perhaps three miles, but by river it is almost seven. The Thames, in fact, having lately steered north-west, now turns south-west, then north-west again, and finally due south, with a brief south-westerly phase at Great Marlow. And throughout the entire voyage not one trading vessel has appeared; yet Cookham a century ago was served by scores of barges every week, some of them bound for Oxford, others going down-stream to London. In among them were sailing boats and rowing boats making for the nearest shop, pub, church, smithy; with here and there a family rowing for tea with friends, or returning home by moonlight after supper with relatives.

Further back yet, in 1766, our own boat would have been jostled by every kind of craft—wherries listing under a cargo of apples, long-boats bearing bread, sailing boats towing laden dinghies, horse-barges gunwale-deep with coal, cabbage, corn, linen, tea, books, beds, bricks, metals . . . any and all the impedimenta of all and any ways by which men earn their daily bread.

The locks would have buzzed with gossips whispering a rumour up-river, or bearing away the scandal, politics, and cost-of-living-index newly arrived from Wapping, Hampton Court, Windsor Castle. And to the hubbub of humanity was added a metallic music from the smiths whose forges lined the river, ready to shoe a horse, repair a rudder, and (if the palm were well-greased) to oblige any gentleman who arrived after dark, with a pair of handcuffs on his wrists.

Some things, however, have not changed—the cattle, for instance. So far astern as Teddington we saw market gardens and a few sheep, but at Cookham the riverside pastures support considerable herds. Ploughs begin to appear, and in summer the pleasantries of hay-making while the sun shines. Not yet are we in deep country, but suburbia lies behind, and even the tentacles of Greater London have lost their grip. Site-seeing is about to become sight-seeing. One may start by exploring Cookham Dean, which can be reached via a road across the railway. It is an agreeable maze of steep lanes and woods, interspersed with a few old houses and many innocuous new ones. Cookham Dean may have taken its name from Osbert de la Dene who in 1220 held the lands here; but since Dean means, among other things, a valley, Osbert may have taken his name from the place.

At Cookham Dean an official of the Bank of England undertook a labour of love. Some years previously he had been in the habit of telling a fairytale to his small son at bedtime each night, making it up as he went along, and continuing it in a series of letters when he was away from home. Then the child died, and the stricken father thought no more of fairies. It so happened, however, that the child's governess had kept the fairytale letters; and at Cookham Dean, on her suggestion, the father made them into a book, which is called *The Wind In The Willows*.

On London River it was Holst; at Windsor it was Elgar; between Cookham and Cliveden the *motif* is Delius, especially at nightfall, when this reach tempts one to become as Delius was— steeped in the introspective tears of the beauty of things whose epitaph Yeats carved:

> Man is in love, and loves what vanishes;
> What more is there to say?

In deeper country, the medieval country above Oxford, the country of an England that was young, some will feel that there is a great deal more to say, and that neither Yeats nor Delius were the men to declare it, because it was not in them. But at Cliveden England is young no longer; it is sophisticated. One overhears the diners, rising from the card table, or coming in from the terrace, summoning the carriage that shall return them to Mayfair in time to go to bed by dawnlight.

Cookham Lock, by the way, is an excellent place from which to enjoy an intimate glimpse of yet another feature of the portrait —the steamers which ply between Windsor and Oxford. These offer an admirable compromise for people who seek something more than an afternoon on the river, but do not wish to undertake a full-scale exploration. From Windsor to Reading takes a whole day, as does the voyage from Reading to Oxford. Since the steamers can be boarded at any of the locks, the voyage may be timed-to-measure. The passengers are amiable, orderly, and quiet. The crew is assorted. One skipper will have sailed the seven seas; another may assure you that he has sailed eight; and sometimes the helm will be taken by a youth who carries in his pocket a Homer or a physics textbook (this being his way of investing the long vacation). Picturesque young ladies serve booze and beverage from a bar below. In some steamers the ticket-collector prefers to be known as the Purser; in others, the most influential member of the crew is an elderly woman. The charges are moderate, and in late spring or early autumn the atmosphere on board achieves a genuine *camaraderie*, especially when it is raining, and only the helmsman absents himself from the tea urn.

If you set out to reach Cookham Lock by land, it is unlikely that you will arrive there, because the lock is very isolated, and no one at Cookham quite knows how to get there, unless by water. Even the oldest Cookhamite will point vaguely at the river, saying, "There is a way, but I don't know whether he minds." My own experience is, you never do discover whether he minds, nor even who he is, because you never do find the way. All in all, this may be accounted a good thing, for it keeps the lock quiet. I once knew a man who spent months trying to reach Great Marlow, but without ever getting beyond Cookham Lock. That, for him, was the river's *non plus ultra*; and from the lock, having spent most of the day there, he would drift down-stream through Cliveden Reach. One may understand the man's fixation, even while deploring his lack of initiative, for Cookham and Cliveden offer the most beautiful waterscape in southern England. Here London is seen and heard to fall astern. The Thames has reached the country.

V

THROUGH THE CHILTERNS:
COOKHAM TO SONNING

THE country: if rivers could observe, one would assume that this river was aware of its changed surroundings, for at Bourne End it expands its chest, and exhales enough air to make this the finest of all its sailing grounds, with trees and cattle to divert the eye. Here, on a breezy day, the yachtsmen of Buckinghamshire and Berkshire prove that a relatively slow silence can seem as exhilarating as the loudest speed. Standing on the bank, you watch a dinghy that must surely run herself on to the towing path. But these helmsmen know otherwise. When the bow is about to bump the bank, over goes the tiller, down ducks the head, swish sweeps the boom—and, lo, she is away on the starboard tack, heaving among half-a-hundred other sleights-of-steersmanship. They sail, too, above Reading; and at Kelmscot I have watched a lug-sail ambling through reaches that would test even a motor boat; but Bourne End is the Mecca of upper Thames yachtsmen.

Unfortunately, the bungalows and boat houses do not rise to the occasion, so that what might have seemed a sea breeze remains tinged with suburban smuts. However, some of these smuts are acceptable because they come from the single-line railway which (unless they have closed it already) still plies between Bourne End and Great Marlow. It was a stirring sight, on a wintry evening, to see the venerable tank engine snorting like Vulcan, and its brace of Edwardian coaches miming a liner at night.

Soon after Bourne End the river sweeps south-west. Its lawns recede, and the woods disappear, until Winter Hill looms up on the left. Behind it lies Cookham Dean, only a mile-and-a-half by road from Cookham Village, but five miles by water. Here the towing path has crossed from the Berkshire to the Buckinghamshire bank. The ferry is named Spade Oak, formerly an important wharf.

Now Quarry Wood rises up and at the same time comes down, within a few yards of the water, dominating a scene that could vie with Cliveden were it not for an outpost of Bungolia on the opposite bank. Even so, this is a memorable reach, especially after dark, when its portrait is painted by Vaughan Williams in his *Serenade to Music*, that stilly evocation of quiet water:

> How sweet the moonlight sleeps upon this bank!
> Here we will sit, and let the sounds of music
> Creep in our ears; soft stillness and the night
> Become the touches of sweet harmony.

Not often has a river sat for its portrait to a great composer and to the supreme poet.

From Quarry Wood the Thames swings away to the west, where it encounters a medley of islets, and then enters what the maps call Marlow, though I say Great Marlow because to say otherwise is discourteous and may prove misleading.

The area immediately below the lock is known as Marlow Race, and was dangerous even when Water Poet Taylor lived. This part of the Thames, said John Bishop in 1585:

> . . . hath made many a child to weep.
> Their mothers beg from door to door
> Their fathers drowned in the deepe.

Here the river grows shallower, and the draught for boats drops from six to four-and-a-half feet. The headway of the bridges, on the other hand, rises from just over eleven to a little more than twelve feet.

At Great Marlow the first thing to be seen is a truism so startling that most people do not notice it, but until the truism really is noticed and really does take effect the portrait will create a false impression because its background will remain blurred. What I mean is this . . . a Regency man inherited much the same way of life, and probably the same house, as his grandfather had bequeathed to the father; but the quality of life today changes so drastically that within six months an old village may sink beneath a new town. When I first knew it, Great Marlow was a quiet place with a population of about 2,000. In 1974 it was a loud town with nearly 10,000 inhabitants. To wander far from the river or the High Street is to enter the Bungolia which nowadays infects

The Regency theatre at Henley-on-Thames
Riverside *lane, Henley-on-Thames*

the approach to most towns and many villages. I mention these things once and for all because, although they will become less apparent as the voyage proceeds, they never will disappear.

The best of Great Marlow lies along the river and in West and High Streets. The view from the bridge is justly famous. Downstream the church and a foaming weir confront the gardens of an hotel on the opposite bank; up-stream the river curves among trees that are girdled by hills, and on the hills are more trees—the beechwoods of Buckinghamshire.

The earliest bridge at Great Marlow was certainly of timber, and may have been built by the Knights Templars who held Bisham Abbey. In 1642 a timber bridge was certainly damaged by the Roundheads (who compelled the ratepayers to repair it). The present graceful suspension bridge, completed in 1821, was renovated in 1860 and in 1966.

All Saints' Church, which overlooks the river, dates from 1832; its spire was added in 1898. In the graveyard are memorials to John Richardson, a native of the place, who became a circus proprietor, and to "a white spotted Negro boy" who died at the age of eight, having been bought by Richardson, for £2,000, as an exhibit for people to gape at.

Holy Trinity Church (1853) was designed by Sir Giles Gilbert Scott. As well as a Roman Catholic church by the elder Pugin (now overshadowed by the cinema), the people of Great Marlow had a Wesleyan chapel, a Primitive Methodist chapel, a Baptist chapel, a Congregational chapel, and an Independent Salem chapel: all built within sixteen years. *Ein' feste Burg ist unser Gott:* or was.

The Free School (now named after its founder, Sir William Borlase) stands in West Street, on the way to Henley-on-Thames. Nearby are some almshouses (founded for six widows in 1608; rebuilt in 1735, with additions of 1859) and Remnantz, an impressive house which, from 1799 until 1811, served as the headquarters of the Royal Military College.

On the right of the street is the house (formerly three cottages) which Shelley rented in 1817. Here he completed *The Revolt Of Islam*, with which he sought to discover "the temper of the public mind, as to how far a thirst for a happier condition of moral and political society survives, among the enlightened and refined, the tempest which has shaken the age in which we live". The

5

Sonning Bridge

poem's second stanza describes the setting in which it was
composed:

> . . . where the woods frame a bower
> Whose interlaced branches mix and meet,
> Or where with sound like many voices sweet,
> Waterfalls leap among wild islands green,
> Which frame for my lone boat a lone retreat
> Of moss-grown trees and woods.

Those "wild islands" and "leaping waterfalls" are not to be dismissed as romantical gothic. Shelley enjoyed a classical education
as well in scenery as in literature. "I have trodden the Glaciers of
the Alps," he wrote, "I have sailed night and day down a rapid
stream among mountains." When Shelley lived at Great Marlow
the river was less tidy than it is today, and the hills above it were,
by any English standard, remote country. Time has not wholly
tamed the land he knew. Still the dense beechwoods ring the sky.
Still, on the northern shore, lanes burrow upwards into a realm
whose farms and cottages testify that sylvan suburbia lies astern.
This is farming country, and on it old-fashioned things appear—a
roof without an aerial, and old men in gaiters, and children who
never call you "Mate".

But Great Marlow itself is not old-fashioned. On the contrary
it has changed its way of life. Once upon a time the river traffic
here was so heavy that it rivalled the inland route to London, and
for a while eclipsed it. The account books of Thomas Oliffe, a
Chiltern maltster, show that between 1732 and 1739 he was
sending 1,500 sacks yearly from Great Marlow to Queenhithe.
On their return voyage the barges carried groceries, coals, iron.
Nor was their enterprise without hazard. In 1772 three High
Wycombe maltsters claimed a rebate of excise duty on malt that
had sunk at Boulter's Lock *en route* for Hedsor Wharf near
Cliveden. In 1788 Parliament placed Great Marlow under the
control of Turnpike Trustees, not for the public benefit, but in
order to facilitate the passage of Lord Salisbury on his way from
Hatfield to the waters at Bath.

In Great Marlow, along a street overlooking the weir, you may
see a housing estate whose homes are fair copies of Georgian
architecture. If we cannot produce a contemporary style which
blends with the English countryside—and none that I ever saw

does blend—then we must do the next best thing, which is to reproduce styles that do blend.

Beyond Great Marlow the Thames becomes even more lovely because it's even more wooded. It is Cliveden again, prised wider apart, and set down in fresher air. Here the river has indulged another of its south-westerly tacks, over the second regatta course in the kingdom, wide enough for eights to race three abreast, past a litany of historic houses: first, on the Berkshire bank, Bisham Abbey, whose lands were given by Earl Ferrers to the Knights Templars, a body of men who appear several times in the portrait, and are worthy of notice therefore. The Templars were founded by Baldwin, King of Jerusalem, to defend pilgrims to and from the Holy City. They were a quasi-religious body, governed by the rule of Canons Regular under the direction of the Patriarch of Jerusalem. To start with, the knights possessed one horse for every two men, but within little more than a century they had come to possess 19,000 manors in Christendom. The Order was first introduced to England in 1100; eighty-five years later the knights built their famous Temple in London. The Master of the Templars was the premier lay Baron in the kingdom. Without ever becoming so corrupt as the friars, the Templars did lose public sympathy; and in 1308 their Order was suppressed by the Pope. Today the Knights Templars form what may be called an exalted branch of freemasonry.

During the reign of King Stephen, the Templars founded a Preceptory at Bisham; and when that had decayed, Edward III granted a manor to the Earl of Salisbury, who in 1338 founded Bisham Priory. In 1537, on the eve of the dissolution of the monasteries, Henry VIII created an abbey here; and when that too was dissolved, he gave the manor to Anne of Cleves, who was persuaded, by Queen Mary, to exchange it for Sir Philip Hobye's manor in Kent. Sir Philip, the last English Papal Legate in Rome, thereupon moved to Bisham with his two sisters, Lady Burleigh and Lady Bacon. These ladies were deputed to look after the future Queen Elizabeth, who spent three years at Bisham. For Her Royal Highness, it is said, the council-chamber was given bow windows, and a dais sixteen inches above the floor. The Hobye Window in the Norman parish church contains thirty-eight quarterings, and must be a rarity. In the library at Bisham, and while walking beside the river, Princess Elizabeth consolidated her erudition. Tutored by Robert Ascham and Archbishop Grindal, she became fluent in many languages, including Spanish. Ascham reported proudly: "She talks French and Italian as well as she does English, and has often talked to me readily and well in Latin, moderately in Greek." Having become Queen, she wrote a neat poem justifying the doctrine of transubstantiation; and at Windsor Castle, as an elderly woman worn by cares of State, she spent three-quarters of an hour each day for a month, translating Boethius' *De Consolatione Philosophiae.*

One wonders whether any other English village contains the tombs of so many once-famous men. Here were buried Richard Neville, Earl of Warwick, King-maker and King-destroyer; Edward Plantagenet, Earl of Warwick, who was beheaded in 1499 for trying to escape from the Tower; John, Earl of Salisbury, attainted and executed in 1400; Richard Neville, Earl of Salisbury, who, at the siege of Orleans in 1428, enjoyed (or endured) the distinction of being killed by what was probably the first cannon ball from Europe's first effective artillery; John, Marquis of Montague, killed at the Battle of Barnet in 1471. But at Bisham today those "old, unhappy far-off things, and battles long ago" are forgotten. All is peaceful, green, secluded; and from behind that seclusion the tip of Quarry Wood dips a green finger in the river. If you moor alongside, you will find footpaths which climb up into the Wood, exploring Arcady.

Next come Temple Mills. Today they produce paper, in a relatively modern factory. During the early nineteenth century they were used to refine copper ore brought from Wales by the mill-towner.

A Temple Lock, elegant with topiary-work, the towing path again changes sides at the ferry, and the river turns north-west, among several islands, becoming very narrow as it enters Hurley through an avenue of trees and lawns. The name Hurley comes from the Old English *hyrn-leah,* meaning in this instance, "a low-lying meadow on a corner", which is an accurate description of Hurley's position on a curve of the Thames. Part of the village has been marred beyond mending by a housing estate, but there is no need to proceed further than the half-timbered Bell Inn, for the best of Hurley lies within a few yards of the river.

Fragments of a Saxon church survive, dedicated in 1086 by the Bishop of Sarum, thereafter to serve as the chapel of a Benedictine monastery. The refectory and its lawn might be part of an Oxford college. The interior of the church was restored without damage to the high lancet windows, the fifteenth-century font, a pavement of thirteenth-century tiles.

So many village churches wait ahead that at this church it seems relevant to ask a question: what is the nature of the attraction which these places have for those who best love them? Basically, of course, the appeal is religious, which is what was meant by the words "who best love them". But the majority of Britons are not religious. They seem content that a church shall order their baptism, marriage, and burial. Of the millions of visitors to these churches, not one in a hundred thousand could weigh Zwingli against Calvin; and few would recognize an apse when they saw one. Yet these Thames churches may still feed a secular imagination because in them we confront the men who made them. We may reject their interpretation of Christianity as naïve; we may reject Christianity itself as naïve; but none of that can dim the vividness with which these churches illustrate the text of history. For example, the walls of many medieval churches were decorated with coloured frescoes, from which the commonfolk—and indeed Emperors and Kings—gained their vision of Heaven and Hell, and of Earth also as its history was enacted by the saints. In those murals Saint Lawrence burned for God upon a martyr's pyre; Saint Christopher stretched out an arm to bless all travellers; Saint Peter stood at the pearly gates, sifting the wheat from the chaff. Outside the church—and sometimes within its porch—the villagers did their shopping, haggled, cheated, over-charged, told bawdy tales, praised God, cursed the government, made amends, and compared rheumatism. Nothing of note occurred that was not blessed, or cursed, by the Church. From birth to death men were shepherded by a priest. They wished to be shepherded. They expected to be. They needed to be. And their need requires of us a perpetual act of empathy.

Alongside Hurley church is an Edwardian mansion, Lady Place. The original Lady Place (demolished during the early nineteenth century) was built by a Tudor sea-dog, Sir Richard Lovelace, who, according to Macaulay, paid for it "out of the spoils of Spanish galleons from the Indies". Macaulay's description of Hurley remains up-to-date: "... that beautiful valley of the Thames, not yet defiled by the precincts of a great capital".

Macaulay then remarks that Lady Place contained "a subter-
raneous vault" in which "some zealous and daring opponents of
the government held many midnight conferences". In plainer
language, Lord Lovelace and his pals used the cellar as their
headquarters for plotting against King James II; and that was the
moment at which Hurley entered the history books.

One of Lord Lovelace's contemporaries, John Locke, asserted
that, if a government defies the wishes and welfare of the majority
of its subjects, then "it is the right of the People to alter or abolish
it". King James would not be altered; therefore he must be
abolished. Certainly he was the most obtuse of all the Stuarts.
Against the Pope's advice, he resolved to impose Roman Catho-
licism on a people who would have none of it. By word and deed
he affirmed the divine kingship for whose sake his father had been
murdered. Now, of all the People's false friends the Whig oli-
garchy and the mercantile plutocracy have ever been the most
sanctimonious, and it is impossible to assess the motives which led
Lord Lovelace to rebel. He may have been a true patriot; he may
have been a mercenary traitor. But one thing is certain; Lady
Place became the scene of midnight flittings, as peers and other
personages arrived from London, balancing the head they feared
to lose against the honours they hoped to win. Lord Lovelace
staked everything he possessed. One night he and seventy of his
friends and servants crossed the river, and galloped through the
darkness into Gloucestershire, intending to raise a rebellion. But
the Duke of Beaufort, who remained loyal to the King, had
already summoned the Militia, which halted Lord Lovelace's party
at Cirencester, forbidding them to advance. Lovelace had either
to retreat or to fight. He fought. The skirmish was short and not
severe. The rebels were overpowered; Lord Lovelace of Lady
Place went as a prisoner to Gloucester Castle; and Hurley—
assured of its place in history—retreated into what Coleridge
called the "meek Sabbath of self-content".

One of the creeks at Hurley leads towards Harleyford Manor,
a red-brick mansion, designed by the Sir Robert Taylor who
built Maidenhead Bridge. The setting here is idyllic: tree-lined,
tranquil, with a swan or so and a boat or two, equally white and
comparably graceful.

Now the Chilterns draw even closer to the water, and, for the
first time since Teddington, the voice of rural England is heard—

not metaphorically, but by word of mouth. In the Chilterns are one of the few people who really do pronounce "I" as "Oi", so that the sentence "That's a bit of all right" becomes "Thart's a bee or-roy-it". Here, even in the late twentieth century, some of the old natives still say "slommakin" for "sluttish", and "pimmocky" for "fastidious". But the music will soon die, outdated by tele-vised London—Yankeedoodle.

J. M. Synge, the greatest English-writing dramatist since Shakespeare, maintained that every speech in a play must be "as fully flavoured as a nut or an apple, and such speeches cannot be written by anyone who works among a people who have shut their lips upon poetry". Synge, of course, worked among the peasants of southern Ireland and its islands, with whose poetry England cannot vie. Nevertheless, such poetry as the English do indulge is best heard in their country talk, which, as Wordsworth declared, "is a more permanent and a far more philosophical language, than that which is frequently substituted for it by Poets". By means of that talk, even on the darkest night, a man who has mastered its music can say whether he is in south West-morland or in north Westmorland; east of the Tamar or west; in Shropshire or in Herefordshire.

The next stately home is Medmenham Abbey. Seen from the Berkshire bank, Medmenham makes as pleasant a picture as any since Teddington. The Thames here is curved, like the neck of a swan, and many willows hang as it were like harps above the water, as though Buckingham were Babylon, and themselves in tears, not because they are sad, but from a shrewdly feminine assurance that the posture well becomes them.

Medmenham Abbey, dedicated to Saint Mary, was completed on 3rd January, 1200, and thereafter ranked as cell of the Cistercian Abbey at Woburn in Bedfordshire. It seems not to have prospered. In 1536 only the abbot and one monk remained. They asked to be annexed to Bisham Abbey, an Augustinian foundation. Bisham itself was suppressed three years later, and the lands at Medmen-ham passed to the Duffield family, who converted the ruins into a mansion. The present abbey is a mixture of medieval rubble, Tudor brickwork, eighteenth-century Gothic, and some Victorian addenda.

During the eighteenth century Medmenham Abbey became the headquarters of the notorious Hell Fire Club, which consisted of a dozen psychopaths who styled themselves Monks of Saint Francis, and indulged certain infantile malpractices. One of the members was John Wilkes, the professional left-winger, whose last words were his wisest: "What a fool I have been." Compassion is the proper response to the Hell Fire Club. In any event, the Monks' black magic seems dingily grey alongside Baudelaire's quest for self-corruption. By and large, the English make uncommonly poor degenerates. The climate is against them.

A few hundred yards above the abbey, on the same side of the river, Ferry Lane leads into Medmenham hamlet. A monument at the defunct ferry bears an inscription: "This monument was erected to commemorate the successful action fought by Hudson Ewebank Kearley, First Viscount Devonport PC., which resulted in the Court of Appeal deciding that on the 28th March, 1899, that Medmenham Ferry is public." Here the towing-path crosses from Berkshire into Buckinghamshire.

Medmenham hamlet repays the pleasure of admiring it, even although Ferry Lane does begin badly, with a sizeable water research station (this, however, is partly hidden among trees). Higher up the lane, on the left, is the handsome Tudor manor house, and beyond it, on the right, two brick-and-flint cottages.

Medmenham church was built of local chalk and flint, in a hollow where Ferry Lane joins the road into Henley-on-Thames. A memorial names every villager who served during the 1914 war; among them was Viscount Devonport, first chairman of the Port of London Authority.

The sixteenth-century Dog and Badger Inn stands on the far side of the highway. Above it, in wooded scarp, is a seventeenth-century farmhouse of brick and flint.

Whittington House, east of the abbey, is a Victorian building on the side of a farm (it belonged to the University of Oxford) whose rents provided scholarships for poor boys from Jersey and Guernsey.

If someone who had never seen the river were to inquire after a typical Thames scene, he would need to be reminded that the Thames never is typical of itself as a whole. For affairs of State one must choose London's River and the beginnings of Sylvan Suburbia; for dramatic scenery one must cite Cliveden Reach or Goring Gap; and above Lechlade is a countryside as deep as any in southern England. But if the visitor would carry away a memory which, in varying degree, unites all of those aspects, then he may follow the Thames as it curves past Medmenham Abbey, with the woods of Rose Hill high to the left, and innumerable other hills on the right, higher yet and still more densely wooded.

These woods draw attention to a new feature of the portrait—the Chiltern Hundreds—whose origins go back to Saxon times when Leofstan, twelfth abbot of Saint Alban's, granted land to three men who, in return, paid him a yearly tribute of five ounces of gold, a horse, a mastiff, and (more to the point) a promise that they would protect the district against brigands from the nearby Chilterns. Their protectorate became an hereditary office, which William the Conqueror abolished. The brigands, however, he did not suppress. Indeed, they so multiplied that the protectorate was revived as part of the Stewardship of the Chiltern Hundreds—the Hundreds, that is, of Stoke, Desborough, and Burnham.

This Stewardship was no sinecure. So late as 1660 the poet Drayton complained of the Chilterns: "Here, if you beat a bush, it's odds you'll start a thief." The hillfolk, for their part, protested that the outlaws ". . . never were here natives, but fled hither for their shelter out of neighbouring counties". Captured outlaws were hanged by the way as a warning to wantons. Several Chiltern place-names record that fact: Hangings Lane, Gallows Hill, Hang Alley. Fortunately, the times became less violent, the law grew more effective, and the Chiltern Hundreds became a sinecure.

Long before that, however, some members of the Commons were neglecting their London duties in order to fulfil their rural functions as landowners. To stem the ebbing tide, Parliament in 1623 passed a law forbidding members to resign their seats. That law has never been repealed.

In 1707 the Commons faced another threat, this time from the abuse of royal patronage, which was packing the Lower House with placemen. A Bill was therefore passed whereby any member who accepted an office of profit under the Crown lost his seat in the Commons.

In 1750 it so happened that the member for Wareham desired to stand for the neighbouring constituency of Dorchester. Bearing in mind the Acts of 1623 and 1707, he chose to accept the Stewardship of the Chiltern Hundreds, a sinecure worth £1 yearly. Thus the Stewardship (and that of Northstead) became the only

way in which a man may honourably relinquish his seat in the
Commons, other than by dying or accepting a peerage (but so
many peerages have been accepted, by so many sorts and conditions of men, that, on the whole, members do not willingly
embrace a fate which to them seems worse than death).

Meantime, the Thames glides on, through pastoral seclusion,
to Magpie Island and thence to Culham Court, which resembles
Harleyford Manor, but was built somewhat earlier. One of its
owners the Hon. R. West, received George III here as his guest.
They tell a pleasant story of that royal sojourn. The King, it
seems, liked hot rolls for his breakfast, which had to come from
Gunther's and from Gunther's only. His host, therefore, employed
a team of relay-riders to gallop from London, carrying Gunther's
hot rolls swathed in piping flannel. The King himself expressed
no astonishment at seeing Gunther's rolls so early in the day. He
simply exclaimed, "Ah, Mr. West, Gunther's rolls. Capital.
Nothing like Gunther. Nothing like Gunther." In his later years,
when he became insane, the King took a more philosophical
view of such apparent miracles, for he wandered around Buckingham Palace, asking how it was that apples managed to get inside
an apple dumpling.

Still deep among hills and beechwoods, the Thames continues
past Aston Ferry, where Hambleden Mill appears, its white
timbers glistening in sunlight. This—one of the very few Thames
mills which still grinds corn—is both a symbol and the substance
of a feature that was vital to life; how vital is proven by the names
in riverside towns and villages—Mill Street, Mill Bank, Mill End,
Millford, Mill Lane.

Domesday Book, which was completed in 1086, names 5,624
watermills in England, but the total number at that time is
incalculable because Domesday ignored large parts of the north
and of the south-west, as well as several important cities. In 1086,
at all events, some 85 per cent of English manors had at least one
watermill. During the later Middle Ages these mills were supervised by the Admiralty, which had power to demolish any mill
endangering ships or impeding their passage. The Lord High
Admiral probably felt no regrets when, in 1422, his fresh-water
charges were transferred to the Controller of Sewage. Stowe,
writing in 1598, emphasized the importance of the Thames corn
mills, even in London: ". . . there were in Queen Elizabeth's

reign, certain mills erected for that purpose, under or near London Bridge, by order of the Magistrates of the City". By the end of the eighteenth century England possessed 20,000 watermills; most of them for corn, but some serving the metal, paper, and gunpowder trades.

The medieval miller was as unpopular as the friar and the lawyer. Chaucer's Reeve had nothing good to say of him:

> He was a master hand at stealing grain,
> He felt it with his thumb, and thus he knew
> Its quality, and took three times his due—
> A thumb of gold, by God, to gauge an oat!

The "thumb of gold" refers to a custom whereby the miller took one-tenth of the flour as his payment. Since he alone could say exactly how much he had milled, his temptations were frequently formidable and formidably frequent. Frequent, too, were his appearances in Court, though seldom on a charge of theft. So late as 1816 one engineer was writing: "In consequence of so many watermills, the country is never free from lawsuit respecting erecting, repairing, and raising weirs, by which the peace and harmony of neighbours and friends are often destroyed." One recalls what the miller said in *The Mill On The Floss*, when a certain Mr. Pivart sought to improve the local irrigation: "It's no use telling me Pivart's erigation nonsense won't stop my wheel. I know what belongs to water better than most."

Hambleden Mill was recorded in Domesday. In or about 1235 it passed to the Abbot of Keynsham in Somerset. By the year 1338 Hambleden had acquired a second mill, which vanished without trace. The present mill was ultimately equipped with a a water-turbine in place of the old water-wheel. Nearly all corn nowadays is milled by steel rollers, which means that the vital part of the wheat, its vitamin, is extracted for sale to chemists, who sell it back to the public as pills that will combat the lack of vitamin in bread. The average modern loaf, said Dr. W. G. Hoskins, "is an obscene caricature of bread".

On this reach of the Thames you may meet masons who in their youth maintained the mill-stones. I have watched one old craftsman take his hammer and chisel to a slab of limestone, give a dozen taps at selected places, and then prise the slab in two, as though it were a sandwich.

Medieval accounts at Watlington in Oxfordshire show that the cost of shipping five mill-stones from London to Henley-on-Thames was 11/2*d.*, plus 7½*d.* for wharfage, and 10*d.* for murage (that being the tax which kept the City walls in good repair). The importance of medieval river traffic is proven by the fact that the parish of Fawley, in the hills inland, contains a narrow strip which gave its villagers a wharf on the waterfront.

Hambleden village stands inland a mile or so, on the Buckinghamshire side, and is worth visiting, not least for its setting at the foot of the beechwoods. During the reign of Henry III the manor was held by the Earls of Clare, a title that was and still is eminent, for the Earl of Clare was the first among the nobility to set his seal on Magna Carta; and the present Countess of Clare is also the Queen of England.

Hambleden church, standing near to a group of brick-and-flint cottages, is basically Norman, with a tower of 1721. There is a monument here to Sir Cope d'Oyley and his wife (a sister of Francis Quarles, whose epitaph describes her as "To the world a Martha, to heaven a Mary"). One curious relic in the church is part of a bed, said to have been Wolsey's. Certainly it bears his arms and Cardinal's hat. It may have come from Hampton Court—but more likely from the palace of the Bishops of Lincoln, at Fingest (which is only a few miles inland), for Wolsey became Bishop of Lincoln in 1514. The parish register in 1753 states: "James Wise, Bargeman. Kill'd by Accident, shooting ye Lock."

At Hambleden, in or about the year 1218, was born Thomas de Cantelupe, one of the few Englishmen who have matriculated as a Roman saint. This Thames man studied at Oxford, Paris, Orleans; afterwards becoming Chancellor of the University of Oxford, Lord High Chancellor of England, and Bishop of Hereford. As nephew to the Bishop of Worcester, and son of the steward to the King's household, Thomas de Cantelupe clashed with the less courtly Archbishop Pecham. Having protested against an excommunication by the Archbishop, Thomas was himself excommunicated. He appealed to the Pope, whose chaplain he was, but died in Italy before his case could be heard. They buried him in his own cathedral. Soon afterwards, miracles were reported at his tomb, and in 1320 he was canonized. Archbishop Pecham would have remained unimpressed. He had already caricatured the saint as "a man who excogitated malice under the demeanour of a dove".

And there was another famous man born at Hambleden: Lord Cardigan. When he received the order to lead the charge of the Light Brigade against the Russian guns at Balaclava, Lord Cardigan remarked to Lord Lucan: "We have no choice but to obey." Having quizzed the enemy batteries, he said, in a quiet voice, "The Brigade will advance." Proceeding, as he computed, at a speed of seventeen miles an hour, Lord Cardigan led the charge, and was the first to reach the blazing guns. Only fifty other horsemen of the front line survived to follow him. Afterwards, Lord Cardigan reported to the Commander-in-Chief, and then retired to his yacht, the *Dryad*, where he drank a glass of champagne.

A long time passed before the facts of the heroic disaster were discovered and assessed. Lord Raglan's order to the Light Brigade was not an insane one, but its wording could have been more precise. His subordinate, Lord Lucan, certainly failed either to make the best use of his own artillery or to summon the French cavalry that were standing by to reinforce the Light Brigade. Yet not even Lord Lucan was wholly to be blamed. The order had been delivered by a young officer who hated him, who evaded his request for elucidation, and—the point cannot now be proved —may even have said something to mislead him. Lord Raglan, a kindly man, did his best to shield Lord Lucan against the outcry.

Another sort of fame was gained by Major George Howson, M.C., who lies in Hambleden churchyard. He organized the poppy factory for the British Legion.

A fourth notability was W. H. Smith, the bookseller, who became Lord Hambleden. His former home, Greenlands (1604: rebuilt 1853) is today a halfway house where senior civil servants meet senior businessmen. W. H. Smith built a small museum (disbanded in 1959) to contain Roman farm implements, writing materials, and domestic utensils that were found in the fields near Yewden Manor.

And yet, after all, brick is brick, and soon becomes rubble, and never was alive. But the Chiltern beechwoods are alive. "Though we call tree inanimate," wrote Mary Webb, "it is really only man's structures that are so; no living germ is in his pillar, as in the heart of an oak." If anyone wishes to know what the Chilterns are like, he should follow the narrow lane through the woods from Fawley Bottom. It is as beautiful as the Chiltern lane from Turville to Summer Heath. In all England I have found only one other to compare with it, and that swoops down into Crowcombe, so steeply that you need to dig in your heels lest the Quantocks topple on top of you. Having climbed a steep hill, the Fawley lane offers a couple of right-hand turns, past several cottages of brick or brick-and-flint—and one enviable half-timbered house—and thence through even denser woods to an eminence overlooking the Thames. Very little traffic comes this way, even in summer. During November I have walked all day here, meeting only two vehicles en route. There are no villages in this maze of lanes—only cottages and farms, some of them isolated, others amounting to half a hamlet. You may walk a whole morning on footpaths through woods, avoiding even the half-hamlets.

Beyond Hambleden the river changes course from north to south-west; and at Oaken Grove the hills come even closer. Here Temple Island appears, named after the building on it, which was designed by James Wyatt, uncle to Wyatville of Windsor. At Temple Island begins the most famous regatta course in the world —Henley Royal Regatta—where, in 1829, Oxford rowed the first Boat Race against Cambridge, whom they beat easily, watched by a crowd of 20,000. *The Sporting Magazine* stated that the race was for a prize of £500, but Charles Merivale, who rowed in the Cambridge boat (and afterwards became Dean of Ely) scotched that lie. In a letter to his mother he declared: "I hardly know whether it is necessary to caution you not to believe an advertisement which is to be seen in some of the papers about the match being for £500. It is not an exaggeration even but a lie. In fact I have not a sixpence staked thereon."

Henley Royal Regatta was mooted in 1829 when a meeting of the local gentry and townsfolk at Henley Town Hall appointed five "permanent Stewards for the regulation and management of the Regatta". This regatta was conceived solely as a fete to attract custom into the town. No one foresaw that it would one day attract oarsmen from thirty countries.

The first regatta had only three races, and was rowed from a point above Temple Island to Henley Bridge. The present course is one mile and 550 yards. The banks have been trimmed, and the fairway made straight by stakes and 169 booms of Oregon pine. It takes five weeks to prepare the course—a task that for several decades has been supervised by a Henley family, the Clarkes, working for Messrs. Hobbs. The cost of presenting the regatta increases each year. In 1914 it was £3,000; in 1920 it was £8,000; in 1974 it exceeded £20,000. Most of the money comes from car parks, catering, and the sale of tickets to the enclosures. In 1914, by the way, the Stewards took special precautions against damage by suffragettes. Two years before that the regatta had witnessed the summit of its social zenith when King George V and Queen Mary were rowed over the course in a State barge.

Henley Royal Regatta is a masterpiece of organization. Its heats are rowed every few minutes, without untoward interference. This was not always so. In the 1860s, for example, Lord Camoys of Stonor Park, in the hills above Henley, became the regatta's first president, and was succeeded in that office by his grandson, who, according to *The Field*, "seemed to think that the popularity of his esteemed grandfather, the old Lord, exempted him, the young lord, from obeying the regulations". His young lordship, in fact, steamed up and down the course, churning the water, bobbling the boats, unsettling the oarsmen. To a Lieutenant Bell, who halted him in mid-stream, Lord Camoys remarked: ". . . if the president could not do as he liked it was time the regatta ceased to exist".

Persons whom the Prayer Book discreetly names as being "of riper years" can remember when Henley Week was a social as well as an athletic event. The enclosures, the towing-path, the hotels, the boats—above all, the racing—were dominated by Oxford, Cambridge, and a handful of public schools. The regatta was English, amateur, aristocratic; foreigners and artisans were spectators. In 1872, admittedly, an American had been allowed to enter for the Diamond Sculls, but in 1904 the Press protested against further invasion (by a Canadian sculler). The blow fell in 1906, and has never ceased from falling. In that year a Belgian eight won the Grand Challenge Cup, and then, like Old Father William, did it again and again. As a result, Henley Royal Regatta has become international, professional (at any rate among Russian crews), unaristocratic. It welcomes overseas competitors, and feels thankful when they do not bear away the best of the prizes.

Even so, Leander and Eton still acquit themselves like men, and will, on occasion, beat the record.

The course itself is best viewed from the hills beyond it. If the weather is kinder than usual, there are few fairer sights in England than Henley's blue water beneath green hills, and a blue sky above green fields, and the marquees made gayer than Joseph's cloak by the banners and blazers and belles. As at Fawley, the beechwoods above Henley-on-Thames are both intimate and beautiful. No doubt I am partial in this matter, yet I have in my time explored every county in Britain, finding in none of them that sense of intimate spaciousness which proclaims the Chilterns at their best. Follow, for instance, the lane to Stonor, whose wooded deerpark has a public footpath as well as a Tudor mansion where Edmund Campion set up his secret Jesuit printing-press. From Stonor climb the steep lane leftward to Bix and Maidensgrove and Russells Water; or turn right, through beechwoods that will sweep you down into Fawley again. This is the heart of the Oxfordshire Chilterns, and it remains sound despite old age.

Henley-on-Thames resembles Janus. When the buses unload their cargo of cottagers from the hill villages, the place is a small country town; when the visitors cram their cars into its narrow streets, the place is so up-to-date that a wise man resolves to do without it. As with Hurley and Great Marlow, the best lies near the river (facing Leander Club on the Berkshire shore) where a lane leads past some old and gracious houses, and to a street of other, even older, homes. Here, too, is one of the smallest theatres in England, opened in 1806; smaller (according to my measurements) than the Georgian theatre at Richmond in Yorkshire, but larger than the Byre Theatre at Saint Andrews in Scotland.

Henley's timber bridge was swept away in March of 1774, during a flood "occasioned by the incessant rain and snow which fell from the evening of the 12th to the 16th". The present graceful bridge was designed in 1786 by a Shrewsbury man, William Hayward, who died before it had been finished. Its carvings were the work of a local artist, the Hon. Mrs. Anne Daines, whose father, Field-Marshal Conway, lived at Park Place, a short distance up-river. Her uncle was another Thames man, Horace Walpole.

The church beside the bridge is chiefly sixteenth-century and unspoiled. Behind it are the almshouses, which look older than they are (endowed 1547, rebuilt 1830). In the churchyard lies

Chiltern country: down to the river

Richard Jennings, the master-mason who helped to build Saint Paul's Cathedral. His family lived in the town.

The timbered Chantry House (1420) was formerly a school. Facing it, across Hart Street, are some other timbered houses, including the home of Mr. Speaker Lenthall, to whom King Charles I observed that the birds had flown. And beyond the church is the Red Lion, where a Duke of Marlborough rented and furnished his own room, for use on the journey between London and Woodstock. William Shenstone is said to have scratched a verse on one of the window panes at the Red Lion:

> Who'er has travelled life's dull round;
> Where'er his stages may have been;
> May sigh to think that he has found
> His warmest welcome at an Inn.

These lines suggest that Shenstone was a lonely man, and Dr. Johnson explained why: "He was never married." Johnson then added, rather vaguely: ". . . though he might have obtained the lady whoever she was, to whom his Pastoral Ballad was addressed". Possibly; but one doubts that any Pastoral Ballad ever was much of a bait in those deep waters. Moreover, Shenstone suffered a severe handicap; he was, said Johnson, "something clumsy in his form; very negligent of his clothes".

Henley-on-Thames has an endearingly Victorian railway station, and alongside it the most insulting injury which a country town can suffer—a block of flats.

The famous Fair Mile, away on the Oxford road, began life as an avenue of elms that were planted by Sir Thomas Stapleton in 1752. Some of the trees lived for two centuries, which is a great age for elms. The avenue was replanted with two hundred oaks to mark the Coronation of Her Majesty Queen Elizabeth II.

At Henley-on-Thames the river heads due south, passing some islands on the way to Marsh Lock, where the trees and cattle come down to drink, and the towing-path walks the plank of a bridge between the weir and the lock. On the left bank the melic Happy Valley climbs towards Park Place, a Victorian house on the site of a Duke of Hamilton's mansion. Soon afterwards the river bisects itself, leaving Hennerton backwater on the left, like a legacy of loveliness cast overboard. The Thames backwaters lead to some of the loveliest of its scenery. On a summer afternoon,

6

Mapledurham: the watermill

when the mainstream has become overpopulated, one may find quietude within three hundred yards of the hullaballoo.

Above Hennerton backwater the Chilterns recede. The land grows level and lush. The river swerves due west, past another ferry, under an ugly railway bridge, leaving modernized Wargrave to starboard. Wargrave church contains the tomb of Elizabeth Tussaud, a great grand-daughter-in-law of Madame Tussaud, once the drawing mistress of King Louis XVI of France, who founded the celebrated London wax-works exhibition.

Two tributaries now join the Thames; Saint Patrick's Stream and the River Lodden. There is a tradition (I have never verified it) that anyone who swims against the Lodden feels sick.

Shiplake Lock faces Wargrave, offering a delightful anchorage among cornfields and pasture lined by poplars and elms. Here an attractive timber footbridge confirms the good sense of the Thames Conservancy Board. Shiplake village is not inspiring, but some people care to visit it in memory of Tennyson, who was married in the parish church, a building ruined by "restoration" yet redeemed by some medieval stained glass from the French Abbey of Saint Omer.

Tennyson first met Emily Sellwood at his father's rectory of Somersby, high in the Lincolnshire wolds. Miss Sellwood was then seventeen years old, the daughter of a solicitor at Horncastle. The couple were more or less engaged for more or less twenty years, Tennyson protesting that he was too poor to marry; but this may have been a way of concealing the emotional malaise which brought forth *In Memoriam*, the elegy for his friend Hallam. Tennyson kept the poem a secret for several years, and even managed to lose the manuscript in a London boarding house, from which it was rescued by Coventry Patmore. The poem was published anonymously, but the name of its author soon became known, lighting-up the decades of near-poverty. Tennyson's collected poems ran into a sixth edition; he received an unexpected annuity; his publisher, Moxon, promised a fixed allowance from royalties; and when Wordsworth died, in April 1850, Tennyson was tipped to succeed him as Poet Laureate. On that high tide Tennyson was swept into matrimony. He bought a ring, published the banns, and performed all those other prosaic duties which attend even the most lyrical wedding. Shiplake seems a strange choice for a north-country couple who had no links with it, but the choice was thrust upon them because the vicar of Shiplake, Reverend A. D. Rawnsley, had married Tennyson's cousin, who invited the middle-aged lovers to stay at Shiplake vicarage—hoping, no doubt, that something would turn up therefrom; which it did, on 13th June, 1850, when Tennyson married Emily Sellwood.

"The peace of God came into my life before the altar when I wedded her," said Tennyson. The phrasing is out-of-date; the experience is not. Tennyson, indeed, was so happy that, as the bridal carriage drove away, he composed a bad poem in praise of Shiplake's vicar and vicarage:

> Vicar of this pleasant spot
> Where it was my chance to marry
> Happy happy be your lot
> In the vicarage by the quarry.

Not from weariness only does Homer sometimes nod; sheer happiness also may lull the critical faculty.

From Shiplake two miles of leisurely rowing or walking will carry you past four small islands—The Lynch, Hallsmead, Buck, Long—and thence into Sonning, which Jerome K. Jerome rated as "The most fairy-like little nook on the River."

At Sonning the Thames flows between trees that form an avenue above pleasure-craft tethered like swans. On the left bank an hotel sets its white chairs on a velvet lawn; from the right bank a backwater glides towards another hotel with a second velvet lawn and more white chairs. Ahead stands Sonning Bridge, blushed by two centuries of open air life. "All men," said Wordsworth, "feel an habitual gratitude, and something of an honourable bigotry for the objects which have long continued to please them." The Thames at Sonning has indeed amassed a multitude of honourably grateful bigots. But it was Wordsworth who, mourning the abuse of language, at the same time defied it by risking "those arbitrary connections of feelings and ideas with particular words and phrases, from which no man can altogether protect himself". Such "arbitrary connections" will thrive and multiply unless they are counter-attacked by a proper use of apposite words. Therefore I say that Sonning is enchanting, the backwater idyllic, its meadows verdant, their mood joyous.

Sonning stands along a steeply narrow street of well-groomed houses, of which some are redbrick, others whitewashed, and all draped with the seasons' roses, honeysuckle, clematis, jessamine. Their occupants contrive to appear discreetly rich. Sonning is a village certainly, but not a country place. It is Bray, transplanted far from London, though not far enough to make the sophisticated hotels seem out of place. Strong indeed is the temptation to paint a flattering likeness, but Sonning is too notorious to be camouflaged. On a summer week-end it is Hell to live in, Hell to drive through, and so hellishly hard to park at that the queue of cars may be half-a-mile long.

The Bishops of Salisbury had a palace here, and parts of its walls enclose a house that was designed by Sir Edwin Lutyens in 1900.

At Sonning lived the Reverend Sydney Smith, whom one associates rather with the Quantocks than with the Thames. Yet he stayed here for quite some time, in a cottage off the main street. One wonders what the riverfolk thought of a man who, when a silly woman asked him to define Heaven, replied, "Eating *pâté de foie gras* to the sound of trumpets." Sydney Smith and his wife enjoyed poor health. "Mrs. Sydney," he reported, "has eight distinct illnesses, and I have nine." He prescribed his own remedies for all seventeen complaints because, as he said, "The sixth Commandment is suspended if you have a medical diploma."

When Smith went into residence as rector of Combe Florey, in 1829, he contrived to make the Quantocks appear even more fertile than they are, by tying oranges to his shrubs, so that sophisticated London visitors went home saying, "What a wonderful climate Somerset has. Do you know, the Smiths actually grow oranges in December." His letter to Lady Holland, written from Jermyn Street on 23rd May, 1811, begins: "How very odd, dear Lady Holl, to ask me to dine with you on Sunday, the 9th, when I am coming to stay with you from the 5th to the 12th. It is like giving a gentleman an assignation for Wednesday when you are going to marry him on the Sunday preceding." In the years before he became a Canon of St. Paul's, Smith described the countryside as "a kind of healthy grave". But his aversion was as intermittent as Herrick's hatred of Devon. Only a lover of green fields would have chosen to live at Sonning a century ago, or to minister to outlandish flocks in Somerset and Yorkshire.

Speakers of the House of Commons seem to have favoured the Thames. The Sonning Speaker—he is better-known as Lord Sidmouth—owned a house near the river, at which Pitt once dined with Admiral Villeneuve. Some years later the French Admiral met another famous Englishman, as follows: at first light on the morning of 21st October, 1815, Vice-Admiral Viscount Nelson, Duke of Bronte, appeared on the quarterdeck of his flagship, the *Victory*, which was cruising off Cape Trafalgar. Looking eastward through his telescope, he sighted Villeneuve's ships. At 6.40 a.m. he made his first general signal of the day: "Bear up, and steer east." At a little after 8 a.m. he asked two of his Captains, Blackwood and Hardy, to witness the signing of his will, which they did, in the presence of his solicitor, William Haslewood. At about noon, as the French fleet drew near, Nelson turned to his Signal Lieutenant, a Cornishman named John Pasco. "Mr. Pasco," he said (and we have his exact words because they were recorded as he spoke them), "I wish to say to the Fleet, 'England confides...'." But that signal was never made, for time was running out, and Lieutenant Pasco begged to suggest that if, instead of *confides*, his lordship would say *expects,* the signal could be made with fewer hoists. Nelson agreed. "Make it so directly," he replied. And it was made so: "England expects that every man will do his duty." The signal, said a witness, "was received with three cheers in every ship". A few hours later Nelson uttered his last words: "Thank God, I have done my duty."

But when Admiral Villeneuve basked in the sunshine at Sonning, he saw only the living beauty of an English summer day, and the slender curves of a new bridge, and very likely some cattle plashing through the river.

I once saw a kingfisher at Sonning. Its wings outshone the water and the sky; and when the bird flew back again, its breast glowed warmer than a cherry-leaf in autumn. Then came three more kingfishers, like sapphires on the wing. But that was long ago, before the birds had grown shy of petrol. Nowadays they prefer the backwaters. In his *Topography Of Ireland* Giraldus Cambrensis noticed that, if a dead kingfisher is preserved in a dry place, it never decays. Even more remarkable, if the body is hung by the beak, its plumage will change every year, as though the kingfisher were still alive.

It is indeed easy to praise Sonning. Like almost every other riverside village below Oxford, it is a Matins sort of place, to be savoured early, before the sun-worshippers have arrived. The pleasantest vantage point is the Oxfordshire towing path, from which you can see both the river and its backwater. And how slim the river has become. Twelve strokes, you feel, would carry a swimmer to the other side. As the steamer passes by, you wonder whether she will manage to squeeze herself under the bridge.

Sunna and his tribe chose well when they settled here, and named the place *Sunningas*, the home of Sunna's people.

VI

WATER MUSIC: AN INTERLUDE

ONLY the sigh of the sculls when they cup the water, and a rhythmic clop from the rowlocks: there is no other sound.

I watch the metronome of my shadow sculling. It rises and falls along the length of the keel, and sprawls across the thwarts when I swing forward. Sometimes I pause, leaning on the sculls, and then the silence seems absolute. Even the crystals from the blades slip soundless into the water, scarcely dimpling it; but as each droplet falls, it flashes a spectrum; and when a dozen glide together, they carve a rainbow. So, while the sun mounts a blue sky, the rowlocks creak, the sculls murmur, the shadows see-saw.

The Thames this morning is like a pretty woman whom artifice and Nature have so preened that even the painter of her portrait is roused from an habitual detachment.

After an hour I reach a bridge, and rest there, under its middle arch, with a forefinger touching the damp moss; seeing face-to-face the gaunt pillars that never felt the sun, but know only the lapping water and at evening a bold fish rising. Behind is a church grey as the bridge and older. Its tower looms like a wheelhouse above the stern. Beyond the tower are the roofs of a village, and beyond the roofs the window of a farmhouse in the hills, flashing its message to the morning. Higher still, beechwoods perch on the peak of perfection, riper than May, younger than July. Like eagles they mount up and are not weary.

Then once more forward, out of the shadows, into the sunlight, while the land falls away as in a ship's wake, and the hills and the village with it, dipping deeper and deeper towards the stern and thence into the river itself.

Now the woods (that had dropped behind) appear to starboard, this time delving to the water, and in places overhanging it, so that tree-roots are seen, sleeping like gnarled snakes. Willows seem to grow from the water. Among them some midges circle a shaft of the sun, and for one instant the wings of an insect burn bluer than the sky.

Presently I rest again, choosing a tree that is surely the haunt of lovers and other privy counsellors, for its roots splay outward to form a roof above the river. I glance up, between the branches, marvelling how they grow—not rising from a level surface, but anchored upon tiers which shelve to create a cliff so steep that only by craning my neck can I see its summit. From the bank two small eyes examine me. When I move, they are snuffed quicker than candles.

Once again I head up-stream, which bends now in a blue arc flanked by meadows with buttercups streaming in sunlight. Suddenly the wooded banks break, and a rich man's house swims by, glinting white above polished lawns. Then the vision slides astern, and meadows re-appear, studded hereabouts with elms and one cow udder-deep in water, swishing her tail against the flies.

At noon I take my first dip, cool and gradual from a beach whose pebbles shimmer when I stir the water above them. They glitter like sunken treasure, and over them the minnows move, indeterminate as the path of an atom.

During the afternoon I rowed through driftwood in a back-water out of the breeze. There the surface was utterly still, confounding Pascal's assertion that rivers are roads which move. The fairway became so narrow that I kept my head swivelled to face-about. It was as though I were gliding through the heart of a forest. Boughs of grey elm drooped to arch an avenue above driftwood that lounged lazier than crocodiles. Sometimes I had to crouch in order to pass beneath the branches, and once I lay on my back, propelling the boat by grasping the trees. The creek itself was so sinuous that I could not guess in what direction the next curve would veer. All the while, sunlight filtered from dense leaves, and patterns of floating weed appeared, seeming to have been born under the water, never at all to have fallen into it.

So many birds sang that even the steady chiff-chaff was lost in a chorus of thrush, yellow-hammer, robin, wren, lark, chaffinch, blackbird, cuckoo—and as many more as you cared to imagine, or all were present though invisible. And since it seemed some-

thing to make a song about, I did make a song about it, which
I still remember, though I never wrote it down:

> Again with lyric wing
> The birds arise to sing
> While greenly growing hay
> Distils a time of day:
> All over the land
> A magical wand
> Is born to command.
>
> Again the bumble comes
> And through the nectar hums
> While from the pool has run
> A lizard in the sun:
> The season of play
> Is willing to stay
> Awhile-and-a-day.
>
> Again the lambs abound
> With life's beseeching sound
> While on his mounting rays
> The sun ascends a dais:
> By day and by night
> The rivers recite
> A logos of light.

And after that I went on, until the creek narrowed and grazed
the sculls; so I made fast to a tree, and stepped ashore, and lay
down in the sun.

And there I still am, with two books beside me, though I doubt
that either of them will be opened. Today they are Hecubas, and
the three of us mean nothing to one another. Instead, I shall
browse on a different book, between its lines; for at this place,
in such weather, one achieves an insight into Bishop Cusa's
merging of contraries. Nothing matters, and all things may be
more important than we know.

As the afternoon wears on, the heat sends me to bathe every
quarter-hour. No towels are needed; the sunlight is a drying-
machine. The boat cushions are too hot to lie on; a bar of choco-
late becomes a tributary; flakes of tobacco curl at their edges, like
moths among flames. It is difficult to remember that within a few

hours the creek will have grown dark and cool. To remember winter is impossible, for this sunshine seeps through the body and into the brain; and one no longer marvels that men once worshipped it. Like the touch of a healer, it cauterizes care.

At six o'clock the timber of a lock-gate was dribbling its tar. Whenever a window caught the sun, it blinded. The world and everything within the world smiled because summer had staunched the *lachrymae rerum*. Time became what it ought never to have ceased to be—a lozenge on slow tongues.

Such days come rarely, and pass swiftly, but the memory of them lingers, like music in the mind.

VII

A BAD PATCH: SONNING TO MAPLEDURHAM

THE river at Sonning gives no warning of what lies ahead. On the contrary, it seems intent to improvise on a theme which, like the athlete's baton, it has received and will pass on. Here one may say what the homely author of *Our Village* wrote: ". . . nor could a prettier country be found for our walks than this sunny and yet shady Berkshire, where the scenery, without ever rising into grandeur or breaking into wildness, is so peaceful, so cheerful, so varied, and so thoroughly English".

Beyond Sonning Bridge another water-mill appears, its white timber gleaming in all weathers, the mill-race still foaming. After that comes Sonning Lock, famous for its gardens. The keeper here in the 1840s was John Sadler, a Water Poet of the upper Thames; for more than thirty years the parish clerk at Sonning (and an apiarist beside, who devised a new sort of hive). Sadler seems to have taken an overdose of Thomson and Pope:

> Is there a spot more lovely than the rest,
> By art improved, by nature truly blest?
> A noble river at its base is running,
> It is a little village known as Sonning.

There are times when one regrets that emotion and sincerity do not necessarily compose a poem.

Now the towing path on the Berkshire bank burrows through trees overhanging from Holme Park. This beautiful reach deserves its proud title of Thames Parade. A nineteenth-century owner of Holme Park built a school for the Sonning children, which emphasizes yet another difference between the Thames as it was and as it is. The modern State has relieved innumerable people of many anxieties; and for the young it has opened gates which their grandfathers had either to climb or to accept as impassable. Any fifth-form boy can recite a litany of man's inhumanity to man, but the Thames itself refutes the Fabian who would present the past as universally heartless. I believe it would be possible to discover some form of charity—the word means loving-kindness—in the history of every town and village beside the Thames. We have noticed already the rich men who built and endowed almshouses at Bray, Maidenhead, Great Marlow, Henley-on-Thames; but they are only the conspicuous examples of man's humanity to man in ages when poverty and privilege were everywhere accepted as parts of the nature of things. Thus, in 1633 a certain William Allanson, living near Marlow Race, left £50 to be invested for supplying bread to the poor. In the hills above Fawley someone long ago gave twenty-two acres of arable land, still called Poor's Land, whose rents were to assist the needy. At Datchet in 1767 Mary Arnold left £100 to the poor; and in 1822 a Datchet foundling, James Randall, was so grateful for his own upbringing that he gave £380 to the poor.

Meanwhile, the Thames suddenly stumbles on a state of affairs which causes one to blink and then to wince.

First, a power station appears, rearing like a poisonous fungus in the waste land; after that, shunting sheds in various shades of British Railway dirt, followed by gas-works, tin huts, and factories wreathed with pylons and cables which, if they were reproduced in little, would be acclaimed as the sculpture of the year: and above the lot, a cancerous halo.

"There exists in human nature," said Gibbon, "a propensity to depreciate the advantages, and to magnify the evils, of present times." There does indeed, and I have already warned myself against it, with some remarks about country life a hundred years ago; but at Reading the evils have no need to be magnified; they do it for themselves. Worse even than Oxford, this reach is not simply a blot on the landscape; it is a landscape in itself.

What a land we live in, if only we knew. Is there upon this earth another nation, or any part of another nation, of comparable size, wherein exist such infinite varieties as flourish between Land's End and John o' Groat's? . . . the marshes of Essex, the wheatfields of Wiltshire, the nordic no man's land that is Caithness; Cheshire's magpie houses, Cotswold manors, Cornish cob, Westmorland sandstone, Cardigan slate; the Lizard lifeboatman, the Durham collier, Cumbrian shepherd, Kentish hopster, High-

land crofter. Three native languages—English, Gaelic, Welsh—
each thriving, and one of them so multi-lingual that what sounds
well beside the Tyne becomes mumbo-jumbo at the Tamar; a
remnant of ancient nobility, a legion of new technocracy, and
dockers richer than dons . . . shall you find all these in a comparable
slice of France, or of Russia, or China, or the United States?

What a land we live in, if only we knew: and how well, even
now, we might conserve what remains of it, if only we cared and
would act. But those who do care and can act are outnumbered
ten thousandfold by those who are careless, and by those others
who are worse than careless because they would transform a
greenly pleasant land into an hygienic slum.

Now, unless it comes from a Marxist, any defamation of the
character of our economic system is dismissed as the romanticism
of men who would gladly part with main drainage in exchange
for a hand-made chamber pot. Unfortunately, however, cancer is
not to be cauterized by mocking the quacks who maltreat it; nor
is it easy to cure a patient who believes that his disease is the
summit of wellbeing. These miles of riverside ruin are not simply
an effect of this or that economic system. They are, so to say,
their own cause, even as a snowball is its own cause, gathering
mass with momentum. Instead of buying a new car every ten
years, people have been advertised into selling an old one every
twelve-month. Soon, no doubt, even the owners of forests will
pride themselves on felling their timber twice a year, in order to
plant newer (and bigger) acorns. And one of the by-products of
such insanity is to be seen beyond Sonning, in these most of
Golgotha, of unwhitened sepulchres, revealing the inner life of
the average urban Englishman towards the end of the twentieth
century—a scrapheap of bits and pieces and gadgets, the excreta
of Unneccessity. The thing is done now, and cannot be undone
without jeopardizing the livelihood of its victims. Yet one asks
again: what manner of creature caused it to be done, and stood
by idle while it was accomplished? Our forefathers lived amid
filth, and Kings went rank and stinking: but not even the lousiest
of them caused, or could have conceived, the calculated squalor
which infects the Thames at Reading.

Of Reading itself I shall say only this, that during the nineteenth
century it suffered an acute attack of prosperity, from which it
has never recovered. Fortunately, two features of the portrait

appear at this point, to raise our spirits while we plod through outer Reading. The first is the Kennet-Avon Canal, which joins the Thames via the River Kennet. I can remember when the Kennet was easily navigable into Newbury; and if any man chose to pass through 106 locks, he was at liberty to sail from Reading to America by way of Bristol.

One tends to regard canals as relatively modern, but they are not. Herodotus somewhere describes a canal across the Suez Isthmus. The Romans, certainly, inherited a waterworks tradition from the Etruscans who drained the marshlands of Ansidonia. And it was the Romans who built Britain's first canal, Car Dyke, to join and perhaps to drain the Witham and the Nene. But the true begetter of English canals was a beautiful young widow, assisted by Francis Egerton, third Duke of Bridgewater. This Duke (so the story goes) observed the fashion of his day by falling in love with one of the two Gunning belles, the widowed Duchess of Hamilton. He proposed and was accepted, only to discover that he could not endure his future sister-in-law, the other belle, Lady Coventry. He then made a second proposal, that his fiancée should have nothing more to do with her sister. This proposal she declined, whereupon the Duke cancelled his previous engagement, and achieved a catharsis through hard work. His first task was to make better use of the ducal coal-fields at Worsley and Manchester, which he decided to join via ten miles of canal.

Two centuries previously a canal was built to link the Exe estuary with Exeter, but scarcely any others had been constructed since that time. England therefore lacked a tradition comparable with Holland's, but she did possess a man who was able to redress the balance: James Brindley.

This remarkable man was born at the Derbyshire village of Wormhill, in a cottage with a tree growing through its foundations—Brindley's Ash, as it was called. Brindley himself never learned to read and write fluently. He was a self-educated genius who solved his equations in his head; and if a problem proved especially teasing, he took it to bed with him, and would not come downstairs until he had solved it. Him the Duke of Bridgewater employed to build the Manchester canal; and having built it, Brindley built several others, longer and more intricate. A new chapter in the history of British transport had begun.

The Kennet and Avon Canal was not built by Brindley, but

Brindley set the first example in that design; and whenever I do pass this way I think of Brindley's epitaph, as it was carved by Carlyle upon the granite of resounding prose: "He has chained the seas together. His ships do visibly float over valleys, and invisibly through the hearts of mountains: the Mersey and the Thames, the Humber and the Severn, have shaken hands."

The second feature of the portrait at Reading is Stephen Duck, who was born in the Wiltshire village of Charlton-Saint-Peter, in the year 1705. As a child he was set to work in the fields. As a youth, on a weekly wage of four shillings (such comparisons have become meaningless), he married in time to legitimize his first child. Although he could not read fluently, he did contrive to plough through *Paradise Lost* with the aid of a dictionary; thereafter discovering that he was himself a poet. With unconscious wisdom he began to write of the things he *could* read without the aid of a dictionary—the village, the shepherds, dawn, streams, bird-song—those verities which, being eternal, outlive fashion.

Nowadays we are accustomed to *sans-culotte* plays and novels, but in Duck's time a plough-boy poet was still a novelty. Inevitably the news spread, and in 1729 an Oxford undergraduate generously paid for the publication of Duck's first book. After that, the news travelled wider and faster. A parson of Winchester mentioned Duck to one of his congregation, Lady Sundon, who passed the news to Lord Macclesfield, who read some of the verses to the Queen.

One morning Duck received a Royal Command that he should present himself at Windsor Castle. That sort of thing still causes a stir, even today, even in a nobleman's household. One can imagine its effect on a farm labourer. Duck, at all events, found himself taking tea with the Queen of England. He was young, naïve, personable; and the Queen was by definition a woman. Within a short while Duck became a Yeoman of the Guard and Keeper (the pun was profitable as well as pleasing) of the Duck Pond in Saint James's Park. Later, with the aid of a dictionary, he was appointed royal librarian at Windsor. And after that he became the talk of the town. John Gay dubbed him "the phenomenon of Wiltshire". Pope, though he despised the poems, befriended the poet.

When his wife died, while still a young woman, Duck married the Queen's housekeeper at Kew Palace, a lady named Sarah

Bigg; and when the Queen wished him to become a priest, he obeyed and was rewarded with a royal preachership and the living of Byfleet in Surrey. Yet all these laurels turned to dust because the public, having wearied of the novelty, ceased to buy his books.

Had Duck remained in his proper place, which was at home in Wiltshire, he might have written like a lesser Clare. Instead, striving to retrieve his popularity, he produced verses in the Augustan manner, which was urban and allusive. And when the public declined to buy bad copies of an original which Pope peddled superbly, Duck became depressive, and for six years wrote nothing at all. Today he is forgotten except by students of eighteenth-century minor verse. This he foresaw when he confessed: "I have but a poor defence for the things I have wrote. I don't think them good, and better judges will doubtless think worse of them than I do."

One spring evening in 1756 this sad and empty man, weary of London life, haunted by the ruins of his fame, set out to visit his old home, hoping perhaps that by drinking of its well-spring he might himself become once more a fountain. But it was not to be. Duck's journey ended before he had reached his destination. On 21st March, 1756, "the phenomenon of Wiltshire", having travelled as far as Reading, drowned himself in a trout stream behind the Black Horse Inn.

Yet he was not destined to be wholly unremembered. Viscount Palmerston, who owned land in Wiltshire, had read Duck's verses. Whether he admired them is uncertain; certainly he admired the poet's lifemanship. So, in order to perpetuate Duck's memory, he gave a small plot of land to be leased so that its rent might provide an annual Duck Feast at Charlton-Saint-Peter on 1st June, at which twelve men—preferably farm workers—enjoyed a free meal of cold meat and five-eighths of a pint of ale. That Feast is still held, and its toast is proposed by the Senior Duck, who says: "In remembrance of Lord Palmerston and the Reverend Stephen Duck, with all my heart." Thus are some words of Duck himself re-enacted every year, albeit soberly:

> No cares, no toils, no troubles now appear;
> For troubles, toils, and cares are drowned in beer.

Yet Reading is not wholly Golgotha, for here was born Sir

Chiltern cottage near Skirmett
Backwater at Pangbourne

Thomas White, who founded Saint John's College, Oxford (in 1555) and Merchant Taylors' School (in 1568); endowing each with scholarships that helped to enthrone two successive Primates of All England—Archbishop Laud (himself born at Reading, and a scholar of Saint John's) and Archbishop Juxon (scholar of Merchant Taylors', and the friend of King Charles I, to whom he ministered on the scaffold).

By this time the worst of Reading lies astern, and the river turns south-west, past a former corn-mill, through the suburb of Caversham, which sprawls like Henry James's definition of the novel as "an amorphous invertebrate". It is possible that Caversham possesses numerous treasures of antiquity, but I doubt it so strongly that I have never been there to find out.

Soon after Caversham the river regains its spirits. Quietness comes home. Trees reappear, like mushrooms in the morning. Busy-ness is as usual among the birds, rabbits, cattle, and whatever other creatures claim the Thames for habitat—especially the fishes, which here give their name to a reach called The Fisheries. And among this new-found peaceableness a traveller will recollect that it is with Reading as it was with Maidenhead—no slight has been offered against the people for whom that place is dear because it is their home.

Presently the open meadows are barred by woods, and above them a chimney stack appears, and then more chimney stacks, not as they exist at Reading, but as they were made four centuries ago, to blend with whatever happened to be in sight. Below the chimneys are lawns and rubric walls, so that you might fancy yourself back at Hampton Court, passing some quarter of the Palace which had eluded your first visitation. But this is not Hampton in Middlesex; it is Mapledurham in Oxfordshire, a classic place and famous for its beauty.

Or were we mistaken? Suddenly a litter of bungalows is seen, pitiful as the village idiot. Have we arrived too late? Was Mapledurham doomed before we came?

A wooded island swings into view, and behind it lies the answer.

7

At Whitchurch

VIII

HALCYON DAYS: MAPLEDURHAM TO GORING

AND what is the answer? The reply is a question, partly hidden by the obvious fact that Mapledurham has not been spoiled. On the contrary, it is the best-conserved of all the famous villages below Kelmscot. This is remarkable. One would suppose that any such place within a mile or two of Reading must have become a week-end car park. In fact, Mapledurham on a fine Sunday can be as quiet as on a vile Monday. Had it been possible, I would have passed the place without naming it.

Mapledurham, which is accessible only via a steep lane on the Oxfordshire bank, is so small that even "hamlet" seems a courtesy title. It has no shop, no pub, no post office: only the church, the House, a vicarage, a mill, and some ancient homes. During the Middle Ages there were two manors here, of Mapledurham Gurney and Mapledurham Chazey, each named after its lord (the prefix "Mapledurham" means "a settlement among maples by the stream"). In 1490 Mapledurham Gurney was acquired by the Blounts of Iver in Buckinghamshire, and in 1582 it was joined with Mapledurham Chazey. The Blounts, a Roman Catholic family, held the manor until 1947, when it passed, through the female line, to a great-grandson of Michael Blount.

The church stands within a few yards of Mapledurham House, probably on the site of the original manor chapel, which was itself a part of the medieval manor house. Dedicated to Saint Margaret, it was restored in 1863, but managed to survive. Among its features are a Norman font, a brass to a fourteenth-century lord of the manor, and the tomb of Sir Richard Blount (*obit* 1628) and his wife Cicely. But the most remarkable object is the Blount aisle, which belongs to that family, not to the church. Built by Sir Robert Bardolf as his family chapel, this aisle has been owned by the Blounts since 1490, and is nowadays kept locked by their successors. In other words, part of an English parish church is owned by a Roman Catholic. This anomaly was disputed by the vicar, a century ago, but the Chancellor of the Diocese of Oxford decided in favour of it on the grounds that the Blounts had enjoyed an exclusive user for centuries, that they had kept the aisle in good repair, and that they alone possessed a key to it. The last burial in the aisle—that of Michael Henry Mary Blount—took place in 1874, and was conducted by the vicar, Edward Coleridge, a nephew of the poet. Mapledurham, indeed, has had several eminent vicars: a chaplain to Charles I, a future Bishop of Exeter, a chaplain to George III, a future Archbishop of Canterbury, and a Vice-Provost and a Headmaster of Eton College (since 1484 the College has held the advowson). But the most illustrious incumbent was Lord Augustus Fitz-Clarence, who had been trained as a naval officer, but quit the sea and entered the Church to please his father—also a naval officer and soon to become King William IV.

Lord Augustus Fitz-Clarence was the fifth son, and one of ten children, of an actress, Mrs. Jordan, and the then Duke of Clarence. At the age of twenty-four he chose to become vicar of this isolated parish. Perhaps it was the isolation which attracted him. Certainly he had difficulty in obtaining it, for the vicar did not wish to leave, and had to be persuaded by the King, who made him Bishop of Chester, and then translated him to the Archbishopric of Canterbury. The King's son, at all events, ministered here from 1829 until his death in 1854, when he was buried in the churchyard, under a yew tree, with an epitaph which describes him as he essentially was: "Augustus Fitz-Clarence, vicar of Mapledurham." Yet his uneventful life did contain one high occasion, when he preached to his own father, in Bushy church, on the morning after the father's accession to the throne. One hopes that His Majesty went away feeling better, even if he did not quite manage to become so.

Mapledurham House was built in 1588, in the then-fashionable shape of an E; having mullioned windows, pointed gables, and bricks so weathered that they appear to move along the spectrum, being sometimes scarlet, sometimes pink. The House has entertained two eminent guests; a Queen and a poet. The former was the late Queen Mary, a personal friend of Mr. and Mrs. Riddell Blount, who then resided there. The poet was Alexander Pope.

Pope's love for the Blount sisters is among the romances of literature. He first met the two girls at the home of a mutual friend, Anthony Englefield; Pope being then nineteen, and they —Martha and Teresa Blount—respectively seventeen and nineteen. Unlike most girls, they were undeterred by the fact that Pope was four feet and six inches high, with a limp and a deformed spine. To begin with, Pope seems to have favoured Teresa, but came to prefer the sister, whom he loved throughout the rest of his life. "Patty", he called her, and at times of stress turned to her for comfort. "My poor father died last night," he wrote. "Believe me, since I do not forget you now, I never shall. . . ." When Patty contracted smallpox, Pope assured her parents: ". . . whatever the ravages a merciless distemper may commit, I dare promise her boldly . . . she shall have one man as much her admirer as ever."

It is pleasant to know that this youth, who was to become so venemous, enjoyed at Mapledurham the felicities of flirting with two pretty girls. Imagination sees them by the river, arm in arm; or at the mill, earnestly discussing the life of which they knew so little; or among the woods that share their laughter with an echo. Such moments may have returned to Pope when he spoke his dying words: "There is nothing that is meritorious but virtue and friendship; and, indeed, friendship itself is but a part of virtue."

Mapledurham watermill stands—perhaps one should say sleeps —within a couple of hundred yards of the church, fringed there by trees, meditating on the backwater that once served it. This is not the most impressive mill on the Thames, but to me it seems the most beautiful. To sit here on a summer afternoon, sampling the quiet sounds of a river one cannot see, is to understand why Constable, a miller's son, confessed himself happiest "when surrounded by weirs, backwaters, nets and willows, with the smell of weeds, flowing water and flour in my nostrils".

There is a street at Mapledurham, though it would seem less misleading to say that at Mapledurham the narrow lane comes to an end; and just before it does end, it passes a group of almshouses that were built by Sir Richard Blount in 1614, with money provided by his kinsman, Sir Charles Lyster. A little above them is a cottage with a varied career, for having started life as the priest's house, it became a public house (King's Arms) and is now a private house (White House).

Nearby stands the old Forge Cottage, erected in 1691. This, like the Thames water-mills, is a feature of the portrait which deserves attention.

Until the closing years of the nineteenth century every Thames wharf, and most of the river villages, had a smithy. Not by chance is Smith the commonest name in any telephone directory. Even in Scotland the Smiths far outnumber the MacGregors and MacDonalds. Place-names, too, bear the smith's imprint—Smeetham in Kent, Hammersmith in Middlesex, Smeaton in Yorkshire, Smethcote in Shropshire, Smethwick in Cheshire. And the Thames countryside bears another testimony to its smiths—the Blacksmiths Arms, for example, and the Three Horseshoes, taken from the arms of the Farriers' Company, which show two horses supporting "argent, three horsehoss sable, pierced of the field", above the motto *Vi et Virtute* or Brawn and Integrity.

As early as the fourteenth century the Thames farriers had their own fraternity, but their most venerable spokesman today is the Worshipful Company of Farriers, which received its charter from Charles II in order that it might raise the standards of craftsmanship, and "apprehend every misdemeanor and defective workes and medicines to the intent that due and legall prosecution be had and taken against all and every such offenders".

The riverside farrier has disappeared forever, ousted by the nearest garage. But he has not disappeared from the country of the Thames. On the contrary, by acquiring new skills—notably at welding—the modern farrier is meeting new demands. Instead of relying on horses (of which there are less than 200,000 in Britain) he looks to farm machines and implements. I know of one Chiltern forge which closed during the 1930s and was idle for thirty years. Now it has re-opened to ply a brisk trade among farmers and horse-riders.

It was a Thames blacksmith who first told me about Eloi, Bishop of Noyon, the patron saint of farriers. According to legend, when his horse refused to be shod, Saint Eloi cut off its leg, nailed the shoe to it, and then replaced the limb, which healed miraculously. Farriers usually refer to their patron as Saint Loo. He is not included in the English calendar, but his effigy does appear on the rood screen of the parish church at Hemstead in Norfolk.

How much has been learned about the Thames and its folk, by studying at the village smithy. There, on a winter's night long ago, the old men would huddle on the bench before a fire that was the only light; gossiping, smoking, spitting, musing. Today the smithy has radio and a telephone. Yet some old things abide . . . the tinkle of a hammer on the anvil, the sudden shower of sparks, the horse patiently untroubled by its acrid hoof-smoke, and—from those old men's ageing sons—the same immemorial talk of crops, weather, time-passing, and the price of beer.

I began this chapter by answering one question with another: will Mapledurham remain unspoiled? No one can say. In 1966, for instance, I was shown some sticks of wood, tied together with string, marking an area between the church and the mill. This barricade (said my informant) was the House's way of announcing that the area would become a car park when the House opened itself to paying visitors. Access to the river was blocked by barbed wire. The water-mill needed first-aid. The villagers had applied for help from the National Trust and from the Council for the Preservation of Rural England, but without success. Such are the facts and the prospects as they were given to me by a friend of Mapledurham.

On the eve of 1966 the Chilterns were formally declared to be an area of outstanding natural beauty, and local authorities were empowered and required to conserve them. Mapledurham itself never will be conserved until it is set out of bounds to casual traffic. If people wish to visit the place, let them leave their vehicle on the main road, and benefit themselves and Mapledurham by walking a mile downhill through woods.

At present, Mapledurham still shares this in common with Cliveden, that what comes after sustains what went before. Whenever I walk from here into Whitchurch I tell myself that this is the finest reach of the Chiltern Thames. The trees, it is true, seem at last to have forsaken the river, but that is not so. They have chosen to retreat, the better to advance. Bolton Wood, in fact, bends with the river, and the half mile or so of level fields that separate the Oxfordshire hills from the water serves as a foreground to heighten their height.

Across these fields an ancient right of way leads from Mapledurham to Hardwick House, which stands back from the river, at the foot of the hills. This roseate mansion contains parts of an

earlier house that was built during the reign of Richard II, with
some Caroline additions and a twentieth-century wing already
merged by mellowing. The Hardwyckes were lords here in 1066,
and continued so until 1526, when, the family having died out,
their house was bought by Sir Richard Lybbe, Server to Queens
Mary and Elizabeth, who entertained the latter at his new home.
Like Mapledurham, Hardwick stood fast for King Charles I, and
was severely wounded.

In 1647, when the King was a prisoner at Caversham, he made
several journeys along the Thames: one was to Maidenhead,
where he was granted a short interview with some of his children;
another was to Hardwick House, as guest of the Lybbes. Tradition
says that the King enjoyed playing bowls at a tavern near Collins
End, on the fringe of Holly Copse above the House.

The Lybbes held the land here until 1909, when it passed by
marriage into a family named Powys; and during the second
half of the eighteenth century a Mrs. Caroline Lybbe-Powys kept
a diary of daily life there. Such records are the most intimate kind
of history. For example, a Miss Harriet Hewett, daughter of a
farmer at Goring Heath, filled three exercise books with news of
life at Mapledurham between 1844 and 1853, which she enlivened
—or at any rate uplifted—with summaries of sermons by Lord
Augustus Fitz-Clarence. Historians tend to neglect the common
people. Such people scarcely at all influence the history of ideas,
and to a scholarly mind they seem unprofitable. Yet an analysis
of the effects of climate and bad harvests would prove that the
price of bread and the incidence of plague were at least as
influential as Warwick the Kingmaker.

Facing Hardwick House is one of the smallest islets on the
Thames. The Lybbe family built a small summerhouse on it,
filled with flowers, and graciously invited anyone to land there.

For another two miles the river is relatively straight, heading
south with level pastures on the left, and the Chilterns beechwoods
half-a-mile away on the right. The aptly-named Beech Wood
stands nearly five hundred feet up, with Goring Heath close
behind at four hundred feet. On the left bank the approach into
Pangbourne belongs to the National Trust. I once counted
217 anglers between Mapledurham and Whitchurch.

For many years a number of people have been advocating a paved
Walkerway from Teddington to Cricklade, with cafés, car parks,

and boat parks. Such a Walkerway might be justified so far as Cliveden—even into Great Marlow—but beyond that, surely, the thing would be out of place. Part of the pleasure of following the river at Medmenham is the path itself—a country path through country places, sometimes grassy, sometimes muddy. For many people the walk from Mapledurham to Whitchurch would be ruined by an "improved" footpath. Two thousand years ago the poet Martial wrote: "What was only a path is now a highway."

The highway of the Thames, meanwhile, has come within sight of Whitchurch and Pangbourne: two examples of how and of how not to grow old gracefully.

Whitchurch, in Oxfordshire, is all the better for being overshadowed by Pangbourne, its fashionable Berkshire neighbour. At Whitchurch the Chilterns descend to the very edge of the village, which consists of a few cottages scattered beside the steep hill, and a beautiful backwater with a mill and some red-brick houses. Here worshipped the Lybbes of Hardwick House, one of whom, Sir Richard, has an effigy in the church, showing him in Tudor armour. Nearby is the tomb of Sir Thomas Walysch, to whom the manor was presented as a reward for his services as wine-taster to "time-honoured Lancaster" and three Kings of England. Sir Thomas's office was no sinecure, but rather a precaution against death by poisoning. If, having sipped the wine, the taster fell down dead, the King chose another cask. Poisons appear to have acted more rapidly in those years. How greatly our journeyings would be enriched were these and similar news-items made available to everyone who was sufficiently interested to visit the parish church. There are 13,000 villages in England, nearly every one of them having a church, some having two churches, a few having more than two; yet how seldom do they offer an account of themselves, or any guidance to the people who are as much at sea in a church as they are in mid-Atlantic. From time to time on this voyage you will have discovered a booklet telling the story of its church, but not often; and never at all, I think, will you have found any guide to architecture in general. The Church of England has many bishops and a large income. May not every diocese ensure that its churches offer their own biography? May not the churches themselves be brightened by a mural showing examples of church architecture through the centuries? At present, many visitors wander around these churches in a stupor of reverent ignorance, rather like a Zulu adrift in the Cavendish Laboratory.

In Whitchurch, at all events, during the year 1753, a Mrs. Swan, wife of a Reading bricklayer, gave birth to a son, John, who became the village errand boy, and after that a jack-of-all-trades at the London office of an architect. Instead of larking about, young John Swan enrolled himself with the Royal Academy school, from which, at the age of eighteen, he won a travelling scholarship to Italy, spending three years there, studying art and architecture. One would like to portray John Swan as a type of successful Stephen Duck who was wise enough and not too proud to revisit his old home. But the evidence paints another picture, for there is no record that John Swan ever did return to Whitchurch. Instead—like Wyatt of Windsor—he changed his name (first to Soan and then to Soane), thereafter setting-up as a designer and restorer of country houses. Despite a knighthood and a rich wife, Sir John Soane impressed his colleagues as ill-tempered, stubborn, conceited. But of his professional success there is no doubt. He became clerk of the works at Saint James's Palace and the House of Commons, and Professor of Architecture at the Royal Academy (in which post he was succeeded by another poor boy who became a knight, Robert Taylor, architect of Maidenhead Bridge). In 1788 Soane designed the rebuilding of the Bank of England; and two years before his death in 1853 he bequeathed to the nation a notable collection of antiquities which he had assembled at his home in Lincoln's Inn. He and Lady Soane were buried in Saint Pancras churchyard, in a tomb of his own design.

At Pangbourne sophistication reappears, and is exacerbated by the main road between Oxford and Reading. Not much is worth seeing, apart from some period pieces beside the Edwardian riverscape, and an idyllic backwater in the heart of traffic and teashops.

Here we re-meet Kenneth Grahame, author of *The Wind In The Willows*. On the death of his son he retired to a cottage near the church, where he died in 1932. He was buried in the churchyard; but the body was later interred at Oxford, Grahame's old university.

A very different sort of author, Thomas Morton, lived at Pangbourne, and died here in 1838. Morton wrote many bad plays—nobody at that time wrote any good ones—including a comedy, called *Speed The Plough*, which has been completely forgotten except for one of its characters, who, like Godot, never appears: her name is Mrs. Grundy.

On a hill overlooking Pangbourne stands the Nautical College, founded in 1917 with money raised by a father and son, Sir Thomas and Sir Philip Devitt. Although the College gives a general education, it specializes in training boys for the Royal Navy and for the Merchant Service; enrolling them as Cadets of the Royal Naval Reserve. Their ships' boats are moored on the river.

People who care for literature will wish to make a brief pilgrimage along the lane which climbs out of Pangbourne into Yattendon among woods. Here Robert Bridges spent a large part of a long life. Bridges died within the lifetime of men who are still young; yet he wrote always with a quill and with nothing else; and he would write with no quill that he had not cut for himself; and he was a great poet. Yattendon might well have been tailored for him. Even today it remains courtly, mellow, beautiful.

Yattendon is the only village in the world that has given its name to a hymn book. At Yattendon, Bridges and a friend compiled *The Yattendon Hymnal*, hoping that it might sound less prosaic than *Hymns Ancient and Modern*, as indeed it does, though not always so resoundingly as Bridges believed.

The gods loved Bridges so well that he died old, having lived the perfect life of art. He was a patrician, born of an ancient family at Walmer in Kent, in 1844. He was handsome—the late Percy Simpson of Oriel said of him "he possessed the most beautiful face I have ever seen on a man". He was athletic—he stroked the Corpus Christi eight at an international regatta in Paris. He was wise as well as rich—having resolved to be a physician until he was forty, he kept that promise, almost to the year; marrying when he was thirty-nine, and thereafter living for scholarship and poetry.

On his eighty-fifth birthday Bridges published a long poem, *The Testament of Beauty*, written in a style that may justly be called new and of his own devising; into which he gathered a harvest of meditation about the nature and destiny of mankind, and a lifetime's communion with many of the great philosophers, poets, and scientists.

Bridges first attracted notice with a collection of lyrics which Housman rated as the most perfect in their kind. With Bridges there was never any nonsense about anything. Of this book of flawless songs he said: "I went to the seaside for two weeks and wrote it there" . . . fourteen days, to compose a collection of poems of such perfection that, if a man had written them in a lifetime, he would account himself fortunate. Bridges felt neither the need nor the desire to squander himself on anything alien from his calling. He lived for poetry, and in it he survives, having given thanks before going:

> For a happier lot
> Than God giveth me
> It never hath been
> Nor ever shall be.

Bridges was altogether a Thames man. Like John Masefield, his friend and successor as Poet Laureate, he spent most of his life within a short distance of the river. In 1907 he settled at Chilswell, on Boar's Hill, above Oxford, whence he could stride into his well-beloved University. One morning, when no ferryman was at hand, Bridges removed his trousers, slung them over his shoulder, and forded the stripling Thames at Hinksey Ferry: but he himself was not a stripling, for it happened when he was eighty years old. They tell me that Bridges is not nowadays esteemed among those who decree, or who imagine that they decree, what is and what is not great poetry; but when the cackle has been cut, all such matters come ultimately to rest upon temperament. Bridges, I believe, wrote the most beautiful poem ever inspired by the Thames. Two stanzas from it evoke the Chiltern riverscape:

> There is a hill beside the silver Thames,
> Shady with birch and beech and odorous pine:
> And brilliant underfoot with thousand gems
> Steeply the thickets to his floods decline.
> > Straight trees in every place
> > Their thick tops interlace,
> And pendant branches trail their foliage fine
> > Upon his watery face.

Swift from the sweltering pasturage he flows:
His stream, alert to seek the pleasant shade,
Pictures his gentle purpose as he goes
Straight to the caverned pool his toil has made.
    His winter floods lay bare
    The stout roots in the air:
His summer streams are cool, when they have played
    Among his fibrous hair.

At Pangbourne the river alters course, bearing south-west for
half-a-mile, then north-west past Coombe Park in Oxfordshire,
which almost joins Lower Hartstock Wood, near the site of the
former Hart's Neck, eighty-two miles above London Bridge.

On the Berkshire bank the mansion of Basildon Park is just
visible from the river—an eighteenth-century grand-mannerism
by John Carr. Basildon stands on a loud main road. Neither it nor
the church is notable; but an interesting man, Jethro Tull, is buried
in Basildon churchyard.

Tull was born in 1674, son of a Berkshire squire. He went up
to Oxford, was called to the Bar, discovered that London made
him ill, and returned into the country, there to restore his health
by farming the paternal acres. Like Arthur Young, he travelled
abroad as a student of agriculture; and in 1701 he designed a
seed-drill. Tull believed that cultivation—he called it "pulverisa-
tion"—was the seed-bed of good husbandry. In 1731 he published
a quarto entitled *Specimen of a work on Horse-Hoeing Husbandry*,
which he expanded and re-issued, two years later, as *The horse
hoeing husbandry; or an essay in tillage and vegetation*. Tull soon
found that farmers can be as hide-bound as doctors and trade
unionists. The Private Society of Husbandmen ridiculed his
thesis that seeds must be sown in rows wide enough for a horse-hoe
to cleanse the soil between them. Nevertheless, Jethro Tull's
unorthodoxy is today a part of the rural Establishment, and he
was justified when he named his farm "Prosperous".

At Basildon the river's north-westerly course drops south-west
for a mile, under the third of Brunel's handsome railway bridges,
past a pair of islets, and thence north-west once more, to yet
another classic ground, the Goring Gap.

No one will deny that at Windsor and Cliveden the Thames
is majestic, but majesty is not the same as drama, and nowhere
can the Thames be compared with the Duddon (whose source is

encircled by the mountains of three shires) nor with the Dove (whose middle reaches are flanked by a precipice) nor with some of the Scottish rivers (rising as becks half-buried by their own spray). However, such drama as the Thames does achieve is to be seen in the geology of Goring. After aeons of unimaginable preparation, phases of extreme heat and bitter cold alternately gripped and loosened the earth's crust. Hills, ranges of hills, entire regions heaved. Scalding larva leaped up, terrible to see, and then poured down, deafening to hear. Hills became valleys; valleys became hills; and, when the time was ripe, acres of ice began to march, goaded by gravity and the press of reinforcements from behind. Then indeed Creation groaned and was in travail while grinding ice crunched new fairways, in whose train rivers arose, like camp-followers tracking the frozen footsteps. Earthquakes and glaciers hacked the earth's silhouette, and after them the Thames began to nibble. The result is a ravine, crowned with beechwoods, and mellowed and made fruitful by centuries of cultivation. Here even Cliveden seems less than tall. If a man cannot visit the Himalayas, he may still, at Goring Gap, stand silent, as Job was silent when the Lord said unto him: "Where wast thou when I laid the foundations of the earth? Declare, if thou hast understanding."

Goring is in Oxfordshire, Streatley is in Berkshire, and both are sophisticated.

The core of Goring is sound; its setting superb. The culprit is Brunel's railway station, which ultimately transformed the entire region into an overpopulated outer suburb of London.

Goring church began its Norman career as the chapel of a nunnery, traces of which may be seen to the south of the porch. The Norman turret received a parapet during the fifteenth century. Beside some brasses (one of them of Sister Elizabeth *obit* 1401) the church contains a relic which Thomas Hardy would have prized—a bassoon used by the choir during the early nineteenth century. One of the medieval bells has been summoning the faithful these six hundred years. Sometimes it can be heard above the Sunday traffic. Not for the first time one must say . . . come here early, or out of season, or not at all.

Streatley seems a shade less spoiled than Goring. Here, too, stood a nunnery, on the site of a Victorian church and its fifteenth century tower flanked by walnut trees. At Streatley the Romans incorporated part of the Icknield Way into twenty miles of road between Silchester and Dorchester-on-Thames. Some of that route can still be followed. At the village of Brightwell, for example, it begins as a sunken lane, becomes a track, then a footpath, and once more a lane (perhaps half-a-mile long) into Mackney. For the next two miles it disappears, but at Cholsey a timbered Causeway House offers evidence which Honey Lane confirms by crossing the railway and joining the road between Pangbourne and Wallingford. The name Streatley means the *leah* (riverside meadow) on the *straet* (Roman road). Countryfolk who live along the Roman Fosse Way still call it the Old Straight (straet) Road.

The landscape here is best seen from the summit of Streatley Hill, a National Trust property. Hills and farms predominate, and below them the river itself, bent like a blue question mark. This is the last reach of sheer pleasure-ground river. So far astern as Great Marlow the farmlands began to assert themselves. Above Goring their claim is undisputed. Some pleasure-craft will continue even into Lechlade, and the river will look the better for them, but from now on the farming country grows deeper and more dominant. It steals the picture and becomes the portrait. It is the sort of country that won Wilfred Blunt's allegiance:

> I covet not a wider range
> Than these dear manors give;
> I take my pleasures without change,
> And as I lived I live.
>
> Nor has the world a better thing
> Though one should search it round,
> Than thus to live one's own sole King
> Upon one's own sole ground.

IX

PLAIN SAILING: GORING TO RADLEY

IF there is one feature which knits every feature of this portrait, it is variety. The Thames contrives to seem incessantly surprising. It does so on a relatively large scale (as when the narrowness of Boulter's Lock gives way to Cliveden's width) and it does so on a relatively small scale (as when the uniformity of Medmenham is made separate by its several curves, each revealing a new variation on the theme). From Teddington to its source, I doubt that there are any two miles of the river which look much the same at the end as they did at the beginning. Teddington itself, for instance, could never be mistaken for Hampton Court; between Garrick's villa and Sunbury Lock the river is sometimes sylvan, sometimes bungaloid; and who could have guessed that the broad waters of Runnymede would, within a mile-and-a-half, shrivel to become the narrow Cut at Old Windsor? Even in deep country the Thames changes its tune, so that the wooded slopes of Harleyford give way to the level meadows at Aston Ferry; and the old home of Sunna's people is replaced by the new homes for Reading's people.

At Goring, certainly, the geologic trauma is followed by a calm and level countryside, from which the Chilterns fall astern, like ensigns dipped in farewell. Among these hills one cannot always see the trees for the wood; but between Goring and Cleeve Lock, although there are no woods, the trees can be seen very clearly indeed—and touched from a passing punt.

Cleeve Lock is served by one of the oldest of all the keepers' cottages; whitewashed, slender, with pointed windows and tall chimneys. For many decades the Oxford University Boat Club held its Trial Eights race on this reach, as those of us remember who once sweated and strained for a Blue or at any rate a Pink. There is a water-mill below Cleeve Lock, and a Miller's Hotel below the water-mill. The river is oppressed by a main road in Berkshire and by Brunel's railway in Oxfordshire; but to the right of the railway a by-road saunters between Goring and North Stoke.

A little higher up, at Moulsford Ferry, the towing path crosses into Oxfordshire. Moulsford manor house became a hotel.

At South Stoke, on the other side of the river, the fourteenth-century church of Saint John the Baptist has a memorial to Griffith Higgs, son of a South Stoke farmer, who became Dean of Lichfield and chaplain to Princess Elizabeth (for whom Water Poet Taylor devised a Thames pageant). By marrying the Elector Palatine, the Princess became the grandmother of King George I; and he, by not speaking English, tacitly transformed Walpole into England's first premier.

Ahead, Brunel's railway bridge (joined to a later addition) leads to a more or less straight mile of amiable placidity. On the Oxfordshire bank, hidden among trees, is North Stoke, with a gabled house and a thirteenth-century church where Dame Clara Butt was buried in 1936. Born in Sussex, she scored her first public success when nineteen years old. Seven years later Elgar wrote his *Sea Pictures* especially for her.

The fading murals at North Stoke church are further reminders that these village churches were also local schools. Here, for example, are coloured versions of the End of the World (not Langland himself pointed a more radical finger at the ruthless rich); the betrayal, trial, and scourging of Jesus; and the martyrdoms of Stephen, Becket, and Andrew (whose name was taken by the smallest and least sullied of British university cities, on the ground that his remains were carried there out of Achaea by Saint Regulus). The Mill Pond at North Stoke is one more memorial to the river's former importance in the national economy.

Mongewell Park comes after North Stoke, its lake hidden among trees. The Norman church here was allowed to fall to bits; the modern house now serves the Royal Air Force. The Park belonged to the medieval bishops of Durham, who must have been thankful to escape southward for a sabbatical respite from their sandstone climate.

At this point a new feature appears: Grimm's Dyke. Some scholars say that the earthwork marked a civil boundary for parts of the kingdom of Mercia; others that the Romans built it as a defence against the natives. The dyke was first mentioned in a

Goring Church

charter which Henry, Duke of Cornwall, granted to his monastery of Bonhommes in the Chiltern village of Ashridge. Strangely enough, the Lowland Scots used to refer to Hadrian's Wall as Grimm's (or Graham's) Dyke; but this was not an early example of Scottish Home Rulers attributing to Graham what belonged to Hadrian; for Graham is a corruption of Graem, meaning Grim, and since Grim was Satan's nickname, the Scots' use of it may have echoed their opinion of all who came from south of the Border. Parts of Grimm's Dyke can still be followed. Its best tract lies in the heart of the Chilterns, above Prince's Risborough, whence it proceeds via Redland's End to the site of John Hampden's home at Great Hampden. Thereafter the dyke grows vague, but reappears in the parish of Prestwood, from where it descends into Great Missenden.

A quarter-mile above Mongewell Park the Thames is joined by one of the lowliest of its tributaries, the Bradford Brook, on its way to the *brad* (or broad) ford near Chalmore Hole Ferry, where the towing path reverts to Oxfordshire, and is greeted by the Leather Bottle Inn.

Now a number of Georgian houses appear, and their gardens adorn the approach to Wallingford, a place flanked on three sides by a Saxon earthwork, as though to confirm John Burn's belief that the Thames is liquid history. Here the Romans built a fortress which the Danes destroyed. Here William of Normandy crossed the Thames after defeating King Harold (and how uncertain of London he must have been, to travel so far out of its way). Here, by William's command, Robert D'Oyley built a bridge and afterwards a castle which is now one of those ruins that Cromwell knocked about a bit. Here Brian of Wallingford held that castle for the Empress Matilda. And here, in April 1155, a Great Council swore allegiance to Henry II's son (the father himself was only twenty-two) or, should the son predecease the father, to that son's infant brother.

When Domesday Book was compiled Wallingford boasted nearly a thousand burgesses, which was more than Chester, Cambridge, Exeter, Ipswich, Leicester, and Colchester. Wallingford, in fact, was the largest borough in the royal county of Berkshire, having fourteen churches. Now it has three: Saint Leonard's (the oldest), Saint Mary's (largely rebuilt), and Saint Peter's (rebuilt during the eighteenth century).

8

Streatley Church

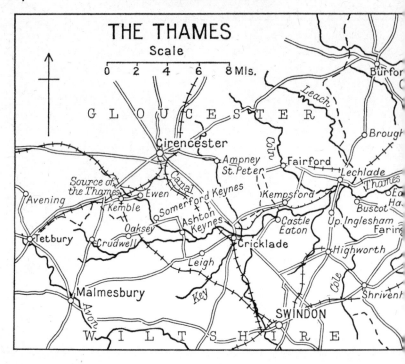

Of Wallingford's monastery nothing remains. Its lands and buildings were sequestered in order to finance Wolsey's Cardinal College, which came to be known as *Aedes Christi*, or Christ's House, whence its less formal name, The House.

Wallingford's most illustrious son was Sir William Blackstone, Recorder of the town in 1749, first Vinerian Professor of Law in the University of Oxford, and author of *Commentaries On The Laws Of England*, a treatise (I am assured) upon which the laws of American and the later British Colonies were modelled.

Wallingford was undone by a series of plagues and by the rise of its rival, Abingdon, whose townsfolk built their own bridge in 1416. Thereafter Wallingford's star waned steeply. Today it is a small, residential town whose former importance may be seen in the houses along Thames Street and High Street, and in the Jacobean market hall, perched on Doric pillars.

Crowmarsh Gifford stands on the far side of the river, a little

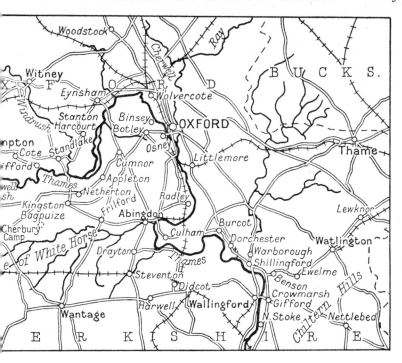

below Lonesome Farm, within a short distance of Crowmarsh Battle and Crowmarsh Preston, whose forenames speak for themselves. The name Battle records that the manor was held by the Sussex Abbey; Gifford refers to a Norman lord, Walter Gifford (or Giffard), whose prototype probably ate and drank even above the normal excess, since *gufard* is an Old French word meannig "bloated". Walter Giffard, Sire de Longueville, was Standard-Bearer to Duke William in Normandy, and although he proved too old to fight at Hastings, two of his sons did join that battle. One of them became Justiciar of England, Earl of Buckingham, and a Commissioner of Domesday Book. His direct and proven descendant during the 1960s was Mr. Thomas Gifford, twenty-seventh squire of Chillington Hall, Staffordshire.

Crowmarsh Gifford was once a leper colony. The church has a vestry door bearing various brunts, said to have been caused either by royalist cannon balls shot from Wallingford Castle during the Civil Wars or by Roundhead muskets.

At this point the river turns from north-west to south-west, studded thickly with willows, and divided from Bensington by the main London road. Nowadays they call this village Benson, but I say Bensington because that is its proper name.

Bensington is still a pleasant place, with three eighteenth-century inns and some red-brick houses. The church, much restored, has a Georgian tower; in its graveyard lies a Sussex man, William Dines, who speeded the process which we quaintly call the Conquest of Space. From Pyrton Hill nearby, this William Dines sent up kites and balloons carrying instruments to record conditions in Inner Space.

Bensington's three inns testify to its importance as a coaching post. Indeed, the villagers lived by building coaches, and afterwards kept up-to-date by building railway carriages. A pleasant lane leads from Bensington to Ewelme, which is pronounced U-elm.

Of all the villages lying on or near to the Thames, Ewelme may be the most beautiful, and is certainly, for its size, the most richly endowed with ancient buildings. It stands on the westernmost scar of the Chilterns, and takes its name from the Old English *aewielm*, meaning either the source of a river or, as at Ewelme, a spring. This spring feeds the village water-cress industry. In 1428 the manor of Ewelme escheated to the Crown, by which, in the person of Henry VIII, it was merged as an honour within that of Wallingford. This honour Edward VI conveyed to his sister, who became Queen Elizabeth I (a path above the common is called Queen Elizabeth's Walk). Here, too, Henry VIII spent his honeymoon with Catherine Howard (a part of the watercress beds is called King's Pool).

Almost every building in Ewelme is old; many are very old. The setting is idyllic, for Ewelme stands on a hill among hills, so that from the summit of the village you look down on a *diminuendo* of weathered roofs, with trees branching from their crevices, and a murmur of water meditating throughout.

Ewelme is linked with two great families, the Chaucers and the de la Poles. Thomas Chaucer, the poet's son, was an official of the royal household, Speaker of the House of Commons, and a warrior proven on the field of Agincourt. He acquired Ewelme by marrying its heiress, Matilda, with whom he was buried in the church. Their daughter, Alice Chaucer, still dominates the village.

Alice Chaucer's life resembles a fairy tale. While still a child, she was married to one John Phelips, who died at the seige of Harfleur. After a brief widowhood the child was married again, to the Earl of Salisbury; and within a few months he, too, died, at the seige of Orleans. For ten years or so the Countess of Salisbury remained a widow. Then she married William de la Pole, Duke of Suffolk.

The de la Poles are a vivid instance of that fluidity of English medieval society which was to preserve the kingdom against the excesses of a French Revolution. In the reign of Edward III a William Pole, merchant, became the first Mayor of Kingston-upon-Hull. William's son, a London wool stapler, waxed so rich that he was able to refill the King's lean coffers, in return receiving the honour of Knight Banneret. Within fifty years one of his descendants had become Earl of Suffolk, Knight of the Garter, Lord High Chancellor of England . . . an example of the "hurly-burly innovation" that was anathema to Shakespeare's Philip Faulconbridge. A later de la Pole married the sister of Richard III; another married a niece of Edward IV; a third, Reginald, became Cardinal, dying in 1558.

Meantime, after thirteen childless years of marriage, Alice Chaucer gave birth to a son, John, who would have become King John II of England, had not another great family turned its coat at the crucial moment of a decisive battle. As it was, the child's father died seven years later, murdered at sea by political enemies. So, Alice Chaucer, Dowager Duchess of Suffolk, was widowed for a third time, and a widow she remained, though she lived long enough to learn that Richard III had chosen her son as his heir, shortly before the Battle of Bosworth.

Ewelme's principal buildings are the church, the almshouse, the school.

The first church here, dedicated to All Saints, is mentioned in a document of 1295. The present building was raised about the year 1432, by its rector, Sir John Seynesbury. It is a noble example of its epoch; a type of village cathedral, owing its well-being to a Ewelme man, Colonel Francis Martin, who, although he was a Roundhead, forbade his troops to enter the church lest they hastened the Kingdom by hacking the carving.

The church contains a sixteenth-century brass to a Steward of the Chiltern Hundreds, Thomas Broke, "Keeper of the Royal

Chilterns". Nearby stands the tomb of the third Earl of Suffolk, whom Michael Drayton named in his ballad of Agincourt:

> Suffolk his axe did ply,
> Beaumont and Willoughby
> Bore them right doughtily.

But the most gorgeous monument is the tomb of Alice Chaucer, Duchess of Suffolk, from which the medieval colours have not quite faded. Four angels support her head; sixteen servers carry blazing shields; and on her left arm glows the Garter.

Ewelme Almshouse—"God's House" the Duchess called it— lies a little below the level of the church, to which it is joined via a covered stairway whose steps have been indented by centuries of pious paupers. With its lawn enclosed by red-brick apartments, this is a miniature secular cloister, a college for superannuated souls.

It was on 3rd July, 1437, that Henry VI granted to the Duke and Duchess of Suffolk his licence that "they, or either the survivors of them, found an hospital at their Manor of Ewelme, in the County of Oxford, and settle a sufficient endowment, not exceeding the yearly value of 200 marks, for the maintenance of two Chaplains and thirteen poor men to be incorporated and to have a Common Seal". At Compline the almsfolk remembered their benefactors in a prayer: "God have mercy on the Sowles of the noble Prince King Harry the Sext and of the Sowles of my Lord William sum tyme Duke of Suffolk and of the Lady Alice Duchess of Suffolk hys wyfe oure first founders and of their fadyr and modyr sowles and all Christen sowles Amen."

The school at Ewelme is joined to the church and the alms-houses, seeming more like a red-brick manor than a primary school. It claims to be the oldest of its kind in Europe; yet the classrooms are light and airy, and adorned with maps and paintings by the pupils.

At North Stoke the unexpected memorial was to Clara Butt; at Ewelme it is to Jerome K. Jerome, author of the best-known of all the portraits of the Thames, *Three Men In A Boat*. Jerome Klapka Jerome, son of a dissenting minister, Reverend Jerome Clapp Jerome, was born at Bradford Street, Walsall, in a house that was demolished during the 1940s. Having tried his hand at schoolmastering, clerking, acting, and journalism, he succeeded with *Three Men In A Boat*, and soon afterwards repeated that triumph by writing a play, *The Passing Of The Third Floor Back*, which was first performed as a modern mystery in a church, but soon became a West End success, with Sir John Forbes-Robertson in the lead.

Jerome had conceived *Three Men In A Boat* as a gazetteer of the Thames, but cheerfulness kept breaking through, so the book became as it was, as it is, and as it seems likely to remain for a long time. The three men, by the way, were not imaginary characters: Harris was Carl Hentschel, a Pole; George was George Wingrave; the author was himself; even the dog, Montmorency, was itself, and did indeed (as the book records) embroil itself with a kettle of scalding water. Chapter 19 of the book repeats Spenser's plea for fine weather, with particular reference to a voyage on the Thames: "Sunlight is the lifeblood of Nature. Mother Earth looks at us with such dull, soulless eyes, when the sunlight has died away from out of her. It makes us sad to be with her then; she does not know us or care for us. She is as a widow who has lost the husband she loved, and her children touch her hand, and look up, into her eyes, but gain no smile from her."

In 1914 Jerome tried to join the Army, was rejected as too old, and enlisted as an ambulance driver with the French Red Cross; but the sufferings which he witnessed in Flanders undermined his health, and he never fully recovered. While on a motor tour of England he was taken ill, and died at Northampton General Hospital in 1927. His ashes were laid in Ewelme churchyard, near the river he loved.

In more recent times Ewelme has set parts of the scene for two novels of the mid-twentieth century, *A Man's Life* and *Sea Drift*. The peace and beauty of this place will touch any man who is not beyond their reach. May Ewelme remain old forever.

In the country of the Thames near Ewelme you will probably meet some gipsies, more especially along the grassy Icknield Way, which joins the lane to Ewelme near a farmhouse at the foot of the hill into Swyncome. Even forty years ago the gipsies were a vivid feature of the Thames. They have received so many unsolicited testimonials (chiefly sentimental) and so much abuse (largely libellous) that they deserve to bask awhile in a brief blaze of truth. What, then, is a gipsy? How many of them exist in Britain? In what ways do they differ from travelling tinkers and the fun-fair spivs? What are their prospects?

The name "gipsy" is a corruption of "Egyptian", and echoes the medieval belief that gipsies came from Egypt. In fact, they came from India, carrying with them a dialect akin to Sanskrit. The Thames gipsies—and, indeed, all British gipsies—are pale reflections of their Continental kinsfolk, most of whom are governed by an elected chief and his *kriss*, or assembly of adult males.

No one knows how many gipsies live in Britain. Having camped with them from time to time, I would set the number at between 20,000 and 30,000. True gipsies call themselves Romanys, and I doubt that any now survive in this country. A lesser group, known as Posh-rats, claim to be half-bloods. A third group, the Didakais, claim to be half-bloods with a sprinkling of Romany. But few gipsies, if any at all, possess a pedigree, and a more realistic distinction seems to be between those who are, and those who are not, self-employed nomads. The latter are few and will become fewer. They earn their living as tinkers, horse-dealers, seasonal farm-hands, odd-jobbers in many kinds. Some of their women tell fortunes, and make mops from fleece gleaned in a sheep shire.

During the 1930s I used to see twenty gipsy caravans encamped along the Icknield Way above the Thames. In 1966 I saw two. For several decades a brace of Thames gipsies called at my home, and were allowed to take whatever needed to be sharpened. They never stole anything, nor sharpened anything that was not blunt. The husband pushed his work-house on wheels—a gaily-painted contraption gleaming with grindstone and brightwork. The wife pushed a perambulator containing their worldly goods. They had no tent. Their home was a tarpaulin, draped over a hedge. During a good week in summer they might earn £7. Throughout the winter they lived in their own bungalow on the fringe of a small town six miles away. Although both husband and wife were well past seventy, neither had a grey hair in their ebony heads; but their faces were wrinkled like a last year's apple.

The gipsies' future is bleak. If they consent to be herded into compounds, as they were in the New Forest in 1927, they will lose their identity, as the Red Indians have lost it. So far as I can discover, the Thames gipsies are either dying out or retreating into the Welsh mountains, the last stronghold of British gipsies. There, like Hereward the Wake, they will fight a lost battle, and few will mourn their defeat; which is a pity because the wind on the heath blows away many cobwebs.

From Bensington, meanwhile, the river dips south-west into Shillingford, which has a mass of poplars on the Berkshire bank, some level grazing on the Oxfordshire side, and a glimpse of the Chilterns astern. Shillingford's brick-and-stone bridge looks well. Near it, the lawns of an hotel come down to the water. Some years ago the hotel-keeper bought one of the Oxford college barges, and moored it alongside as an ornament. To me it resembles an orphaned swan.

Shillingford itself stands on the main road, and is therefore loud, but it does contain a quiet cul-de-sac among trees and old houses, which the children use as a bathing place. The river here is lined with willows, and has a second row of trees inland a little from the towing-path, so that one walks as it were through a wood, while the river follows at leisure, sometimes revealing itself, sometimes not.

Above Shillingford the River Thame flows in, at a point facing Little Wittenham Wood, from which arise Wittenham Clumps, known sometimes as the Dorchester Clumps, sometimes as the Berkshire Bubs, and sometimes as the Sinodun Hills. They are notable landmarks, visible from a scarp of the Chilterns twenty miles away. A curious thing occurred here, and was described by the man to whom it happened—a young visitor from Germany, Pastor Carl Philip Moritz, author of a book called *Journeys Of A German In England In 1782*. While following the Thames from Richmond to Oxford, Moritz reached Wittenham Clumps: "a long hill," he termed it, "with what appeared to be the mast of a ship standing up from behind it. This led me to suppose that another river ran on the other side of the hill. This promised me a view which I would not willingly pass by the way." Moritz duly climbed the hill. "When I reached the summit, however, I found that the whole thing was an optical illusion. Before me lay only a great plain. . . ." But it was not an optical illusion, as he went on to explain: ". . . the mast was stuck in the ground to entice the curious from the road." So, having toiled up the hill, Moritz picked his way down again: "at its foot was a house with many people looking out of the window and apparently laughing at me." Little things, it seems, have for a long while pleased comparable minds.

However, Pastor Moritz soon found consolation in the river at Dorchester: "The country became so beautiful that I had no wish to go further, but lay down on the green turf and feasted my eyes on the view as if enchanted . . . the hills by the Thames revealed their many shades of green—bright green, dark green, pale green—with the tufted tops of trees here and there among them. Were Pastor Moritz to revisit Dorchester he would find it still a pleasant place—indeed, a beautiful one—but the main Oxford road, which is also the narrow village street, might strike him as being not quite what it was. Of all the Thames-side villages Dorchester is the most grievously afflicted by the Great Plague of the late twentieth century—traffic. There are times when it is impossible to converse here. One must point and gesticulate above the din.

Photographs of Dorchester taken from the air reveal circles and defensive works of the Iron Age. Later, Dorchester was fortified by the Romans, who left behind an altar to Jupiter, and the relics of a road. In the seventh century Bishop Birinus built a cathedral here, on lands given to him by King Cyneglis of the West Saxons and King Oswald of Northumbria. "The two Kings," wrote Bede, "gave Bishop Birinus the city of Dorcic for his episcopal see, and there he built and dedicated several churches, and brought many people to God by his holy labours."

The Bishop's cathedral has disappeared, but in its place the Normans and the English raised the present noble Abbey, which is also the parish church. I cannot recall any other village with such a splendid parish church (Lanercost, up in Cumberland, has perhaps a comparable Priory, but no village to go with it). Dorchester Abbey contains so many memorable features that to litanize every one of them would seem tedious and not helpful. Nevertheless, the Abbey possesses one treasure which cannot be passed over: the famous Jesse window. This fourteenth-century masterpiece traces a legend recorded by Isaiah: "And there shall come forth a rod out of the stem of Jesse, and a Branch shall grow out of his roots: and the spirit of the Lord shall rest upon him, the spirit of wisdom and understanding, the spirit of counsel and might, the spirit of knowledge and of the fear of the Lord." Saint Matthew was more precise, no doubt because hindsight enjoys certain advantages over foresight: "And Jesse," Matthew declared, "begat David the king. And Jacob begat Joseph the husband of Mary, of whom was born Jesus, who is called Christ."

Many people, visiting Dorchester for the first time, remark on the extreme narrowness of the Thames as it passes under the causeway, but that river is not the Thames—it is the newly arrived Thame. The Thames itself flows a few hundred yards south of Dorchester Bridge.

Hitherto the Ordnance Survey Map has named the river as "River Thames", but now the name becomes "River Thames or Isis" . . . which leads into deep water because Isis was the name of the Egyptian goddess of fecundity, and one may well ask how she came to baptize the water above Day's Lock. The answer is, she did not. The name Isis came, not out of Egypt, but from the Celts, who used *Is* as the root of their word for water. England teems with similar river-names—the Isle in Somerset, the Ise near Wellingborough, the Isbourne in Warwickshire, the Isk (or Esk) in Cumberland, Devon, Yorkshire. This part of the Thames was called Ise in 1347, and Isis during the early sixteenth century; notably by John Leland in his *Itinerary*. Leland was copied in this by William Camden, whose fifteen years of travel went to the publication, in 1586, of *Britannia*. Camden, in fact, stated that the name Thames, or Tamesis, is a compound formed by the meeting of the Tame and the Isis.

But the Thames, unmindful of titles, continues a slow south-westerly curve toward Oxford, though whether it ever will reach Oxford seems improbable, for it turns south-east, away from Oxford, so that at Appleford you begin to wonder how long it will be before you find yourself back in Wallingford.

While performing this sleight, and a little before reaching Clifton Hampden, the Thames flows past the home of Dr John Masefield, O.M., my old and very dear friend. His estate, Burcote Brook, overlooked the river, and had a small boat-house in a coppice where part of the meadow had been mown to make a lawn. On that lawn a sundial declared that Time, being precious, must on no account be hurried. In 1976 the house and grounds were a Cheshire Home.

John Edward Masefield was born at Ledbury, in Herefordshire, on 1st June, 1878. As a *Conway* cadet he sailed in tall ships whose masts carried sails; in his age he became a Master Mariner. The sea, however, did not claim him as it claimed Conrad and Marryat. Having travelled through America, earning his living at any odd job that happened to be present, Masefield returned to the English countryside, married happily for life, and wrote the poems which in 1930 raised him *magna cum laude* to the Laureateship. Like Robert Bridges, his friend and predecessor as Laureate, Masefield became a man of the Thames. In 1911 he went to live in the Chiltern village of Great Hampden, from which he moved to Boar's Hill, above Oxford, and then to Burcote Brook.

Masefield is *tusitala*—which was what the natives called Stevenson—a teller of tales. He is the Chaucer of our time, excelling as well in prose stories as in verse plays. Despite the years, neither his vision nor his skill forsook him. In his 88th year he published a book of lyrics and ballads which one reviewer hailed as "a miracle of extreme old age that carries within itself a perennial spring". In his 89th year he published a book of prose reminiscences —"a work of art", as one critic said, "comparable with Wordsworth's account of the growth of a poet's mind". There is no rose-tinted-times-past-praising in this man of the Thames. His books have castigated all forms of inhumanity with an *Ecrasez l'infâme* loud as Voltaire's.

At a time of life which few men ever attain, Masefield painted a portrait of the woods that are to be seen beside the Thames in spring:

> We stood upon the grass beside the road,
> At a wood's fence, to look among the trees.
> In windless noon the burning May-time glowed.
> Gray, in young trees, the beeches stood at ease.
> Light speckled in the wood or left it dim;
> There lay a blue in which no ship could swim,
> Within whose peace no water ever flowed.

Tall, white-haired, with eyes as blue as the sea that sharpened them; swift to share another's pain, to praise another's achievement, to encourage another's promise . . . that, for me, is John Masefield, Poet Laureate of England; "concerning whom" (to borrow of a famous dialogue) "I may truly say, that of all the men of his time whom I have known, he was the wisest and justest and best".

Soon after Burcote Brook the Thames passes Clifton Hampden. Until 1864 the Villagers had only their ferry, but in that year a

bridge of six red-brick arches was designed by Sir George Gilbert
Scot, who made a good job of it, providing a narrow pathway
which exempted pedestrians from the toll that was levied on
riders and vehicles.

The best of Clifton Hampden is excellent, and consists of a
few thatched cottages perched high above the river, with gardens
that nod whenever a breeze sways their hollyhocks. The church
stands even higher, on a cliff runged by stone steps. Originally a
chapel-of-ease of Dorchester Abbey, it was restored by Scot for
Lord Aldenham, the financier, in memory of his father.

Two Clifton Hampden people stir the imagination: the first is
Mrs. Sarah Fletcher, wife of Captain Fletcher, who died here in
1799, aged twenty-nine. She was, it seems, a young woman
"whose artless Beauty, innocence of Mind, and gentle Manners,
once obtained for her the Love and Esteem of all who knew her.
But when Nerves were too delicately spun to bear the rude
Shakes and Jostlings which we meet with in this transitory World,
Nature gave way; she sunk and died a Martyr to Excessive
Sensibility." I have met people who laughed at that; allowing the
fashion in language to overshadow the unchanging pity of it.
Had the girl lived today, she might have become one of many
other out-patients who found relief and perhaps lasting cure. As
it was, her husband could do no more than express a tender hope:
"May her Soul meet that Peace in Heaven which this Earth
denied her."

The second interesting villager is Sergeant William Dyke (or
Dykes), of whom they tell a story. One version says that he fired
the first shot at the battle of Waterloo, that he did so against orders,
that he was reduced to the ranks, and that the Duke of Wellington
(happening to meet him near Clifton Hampden) thereupon caused
his sword to be returned to him. This seems unlikely, and I can
find no record that it occurred. The battle of Waterloo was begun
by the French when they attacked a British outpost at Hougou-
mont, held by detachments of the Coldstream and Third Guards.
Another version of the story seems less improbable. According
to it, the Sergeant fired his musket in order to clean it, but chose
the wrong moment.

The Barley Mow at Clifton Hampden is famous. *Three Men In
A Boat* found it "the quaintest, most old-world inn up the river
. . . Its low-pitched gables and thatched roof and lattice windows

give it a story-book appearance, while inside it is even still more once-upon-a-timeyfied". Today the inn is now-upon-a-timeyfied by caravans and an unsightly car park.

As though dispirited by the Barley Mow's fall from grace, the river enters a noticeably flat mood, which it follows for the next two miles, in a more or less straight line, past the Berkshire village of Appleford, one hundred miles above London Bridge. Appleford church gazes across the river. It has a good timber porch above the Norman doorway. Appleford village resembles Hardy's "one-eyed, blinking sort of place", but one of its villagers was very wideawake. His name was John Faulkener, though his unmarked grave does not say so. Faulkener was a professional jockey who rode his first winner at the age of eight, and was racing at the age of seventy-four. The life seems to have suited him, because he lived until within a short-neck of his 105th birthday, having begat thirty-two children. William Cowper, that least equestrian of men, wrote some lines that would have looked well on John Faulkener's grave:

> . . . we justly boast
> At least superior jockeyship, and claim
> The honours of the turf. . . .

Above Appleford the river is crossed by a railway that saunters into Oxford via Culham and Radley. Most of England's ambling by-lines have been closed, but those that remain provide a memorable pilgrim's progress, even although their halts and junctions are no longer a meeting-and-talking-place for the countryfolk. On such lines, in the old days, one met the farmers —cherubically astute, wide of girth, broad in the beam, immense of smile, drawling, curt, dry; grumbling about the weather; cursing the Socialists, praising the Liberals, voting Conservative. With them came their wives—colossally unglamorous, heroically stalwart, magnificent mothers, no-nonsense girls of indefinite vintage; bonneted, bronzed, rougeless. Even the luggage was interesting—a crate of china for the vicarage, new book-cases for the manse, a lawn-mower for the manor, and two trunks marked Singapore, now on the last lap of their journey to the remoteness of an English hamlet. The trains observed certain formalities— boilers were filled with water, and the furnace was stoked—but the rest of the affair was informal. Level-crossings became the scene of conversations between the driver and the crossing-man; starting, as a rule, with the potato prospects, veering to hunting or a cricket match, and concluding with an analysis of the political situation in the Balkans, as it affected Ewelme or Mapledurham. There, on the branch line, you found Langland's "fair field full of folk".

One mile more brings us to Sutton Courtenay and its restful backwaters. Here a twelfth-century building is still a private residence. The manor house was a retreat for the Abbots of Abingdon until the Courtenays made it their own home. The church contains styles from Plantaganet to Tudor times. In its graveyard is buried Herbert Henry Asquith, first Earl of Oxford and Asquith, who owned a riverside retreat nearby, called The Wharf. A classic of Balliol, Asquith lapsed from scholarship into litigation, and from litigation into politics.

Culham, on the Oxfordshire bank, is reached via a Cut, at a point where the river turns north-west, having passed under a bridge that was renovated after damage during the Civil Wars. The church is modern; the manor house is Georgian and built of Cotswold stone, as though to remind the traveller that he is entering a new countryside. Here a training college for teachers was built by Bishop Samuel Wilberforce, an unctuous prelate who deserved the nickname "Soapy Sam". In 1860, at a meeting of the British Association in Oxford, Wilberforce covered himself and his cause with ingloriousness by mocking the doctrine of evolution which Darwin (and, strangely enough, an explorer, Alfred Russell Wallace) were at that time propounding. Instead of agreeing that science had compelled the Church to revise its doctrines, Wilberforce carried the fight so far into the enemy's camp that the enemy—which in any event stood neutral in metaphysical matters—was able to take him in the rear as he shambled past. The Bishop, in fact, was so inept that Huxley, whose task was to refute him, whispered to his neighbour, an eminent surgeon, "The Lord hath delivered him into mine hands." However, it is only fair to add that Huxley himself was not without sin, for when a scientist invited him to take part in an examination of extra-sensory perception, Huxley declined, saying it was all a lot of damned nonsense. Yet this same Huxley had warned Charles Kingsley: "Sit down before the fact like a little child, be prepared to give up every preconceived notion,

follow humbly to wherever and to whatever abysses nature leads
or you shall learn nothing."

The main road gives the river a fairly wide berth hereabouts,
though several lanes and rights-of-way do lead to the towing-
path. It was on this main road that I saw gregariousness run amok
when a car drew up, and its inmates prepared to picnic, so close
to the traffic that one of them chased a tea-cloth which had been
swept away by the rush of vehicles. Then a second car drew up
and likewise made ready to eat, within a dozen yards of the other
windswept party. And presently came a third car, which also
pitched its caravan nearby. So there they all were, like wasps in
a jamjar, harried by traffic ten feet away. Immediately facing them,
a green lane offered peace and quiet; behind, a public footpath
invited them to sit beside the river. Now, these people looked
amiable. They were, I feel certain, kind husbands, devoted
mothers, more or less prompt payers of rates and taxes; but as I
watched them—grabbing children from the jaws of death, cup-
ping their ears in order to converse—I was reminded of Sir
Francis Galton, the anthropologist, who, while studying life in
the North African deserts, was impressed by "the urgent need
of the camel for the close companionship of his fellows".

Above Culham, the Cut turns abruptly north-west, along
Culham Reach—a favourite sailing ground—from which a backwater makes a short detour to Abingdon Lock, while the main
stream (joined here by the River Ock) continues westward, past an
island whose greenness makes a pleasant foil to the rubric splendours
of Abingdon, dominated by the spire of St. Helen's church.

You can spend all day in Abingdon, and still find things to be
found or re-discovered. At Abingdon, therefore, the portrait
must become impressionism, with here and there a feature
standing out because it chanced to catch the painter's imagination
. . . First, the great Abbey (three miles in circumference were its
fields and vineyards) magnificent even in decay, so that it recalls
the Greek elegy "being great, great was his fall". . . . The Tudor
almshouse that became a school whose first master, the son of a
farm labourer, was Sir John Mason, Chancellor of the University
of Oxford. . . . Saint Helen's churchyard, clutching three of the
town's five almshouses. . . . The chained Bible in that church,
one of the first of the Authorized Version, which Archbishop
Laud sponsored, himself a Thames man and Chancellor of Oxford

The way to Moulsford
Village school, Ewelme

University. . . . The old mill and its leet, dreaming within a few yards of raucous traffic. . . . The Tudor grammar school, founded by an Abingdon man in the sixty-third year of his life, during the sixty-third year of his century, for sixty-three boys of his town. . . . The County Hall, designed by Kit Kempster, a craftsman who helped to build St. Paul's Cathedral.

When William the Conqueror spent Easter here, two years before Domesday Book was compiled, the monks entertained him at the Abbey, so impressing him by their piety and learning that he left his own son among them; hoping, no doubt, that he would become a second Aelfric, who also had been a pupil of the Abbey. Later, Geoffrey of Monmouth was to join the school (one wonders whether his former masters swallowed the woppingly magnificent inventions which he passed off as history). Yet even Geoffrey and Aelfric were outshone by Edmund Rich.

Born at Abingdon in 1180, Edmund Rich was forced to wear sackcloth next his skin, to fast often, and to go hungry on Sundays and feast days until he had sung the entire Psalter. Edmund Rich, however, seems to have been perverse; instead of looking back in anger, he advanced with such fervour that he managed to study law at Oxford; afterwards begging his way to the University of Paris, where (it is probable) he became the first Oxford man to receive that university's degree, or licence, to teach in arts. Roger Bacon—whose own erudition waits to amaze us—said that Edmund Rich was the first Oxford master to deliver a systematic analysis of Aristotle's logic. Later, Edmund Rich lectured on theology.

By the year 1233 he had made his mark, which Pope Gregory recognized by persuading Henry III to chose Rich as Archbishop of Canterbury. Within a short while both Pope and King were cursing themselves and each other, for the new Archbishop was a latter-day Becket, castigating the motley of foreigners (who hung on to Eleanor of Provence when Henry III married her), protesting against the King's violation of Magna Carta, and threatening him with excommunication. But a nation is not to be saved by the exertions of one man only. The Papal Legate was ordered to assist the King in obstructing the Archbishop. Edmund Rich's actions were questioned, disputed, denigrated. After seven years of struggle he retired to Pontigny in France, and died two years later at Soissy. Four years after that he was canonized.

9

Abingdon: the old watermill
An Oxfordshire backwater

But St. Edmund Rich is remembered by something less fleeting than current affairs gone stale. Conceived in this country of the Thames, meditated among the spires of Oxford, and brought forth in French, his mystical tract, *The Mirror Of Holy Church*, is comparable with the writings of Richard Rolle and Walter Hilton. Several times it was translated into Latin and medieval English. Though less lyrical than Traherne of Teddington, Rich of Abingdon possessed the same sure foothold among the things of this world. "To live perfectly," he wrote, "is to live humbly, lovingly, and honourably." Amid the noise and jostling of Paris, he found the way to contemplation: "The first step is for the soul to retreat within itself and there completely to recollect itself."

That same step may be taken amid the jostling and noise of Abingdon; but the wise visitor will avoid traffic time. He will arrive auspiciously, when a summer sun is doing the same; or on a wintry afternoon. Then he may find himself with those who have crowned Abingdon as Queen of the Thames.

X

LEAVES ON THE WATER: AN INTERLUDE

THE Common above the river is a no-man's land of gorse, bracken, and turf. It is also the jam in a sandwich whose slices are two lanes, one of which ends where the Common begins, whilst the other begins where the Common ends (and the juxtaposition holds good from whichever angle you regard it),

There, this morning, the autumn bracken seemed downcast and frost-bitten; and the pathway through them was like a cold cup of cocoa, refuting Stevenson's couplet:

> Autumnal frosts enchant the pool
> And make the cart-ruts beautiful.

Puddles were slopped all over the place, and one wondered whether a housemaid had hurried that way with an over-brimming bucket. The leaves, too, were sloppy—spiked upon hedges, like a gipsy's laundry; upright in congealed slime; floating through furrows churned by the tractor.

Beyond the Common I reached a hill overlooking a valley, in whose hollow (we call them "bottoms") a man was chopping wood outside his cottage. My vision of angle was so acute that I saw only the man's shoulders, and hat, and toes. The cottage windows were invisible, but its gutters I did see, filled with rain-water and leaves. Then a young woman came out, and of her I saw chiefly the parting in her hair, which gleamed white. From that depth, through such stillness, her voice arose startlingly clear. She said, "Find me some dry ones."

When I loped downhill, into the valley, the skyline seemed to descend with me, until I thought that it must sink below itself, and, from being an eminence, become a cavern. But when I began to climb the opposite slope, the skyline sprang into position again, and I needed to look up in order to see its summit.

Halfway down the next slope I reached a wood, and went

through it, and came out again, and again climbed, this time over open country. Presently I entered a second wood, which curled across the crest of the hills, like a bronze caterpillar. Through it ran a path so steep that centuries of footsteps had worn away the chalk, to expose tree-roots splaying outward and upward in search of an anchorage. These roots formed a ladder of timber rungs, without which, in wet weather, no one could walk upright. Some aspen leaves lay face-downward on the path, pale as snowflakes.

Six hours later, having walked twenty miles since breakfast, I felt it was time to go home; but the October sun still stood so high that I continued, and came down to the river, and sat beside it, under an avenue of beech.

Only now, during these mild days, have the leaves attained their gaudiest splendour. Already a gale has sent many of them into the water, to be swept away or to shelter in a *cul-de-sac* under the banks. The rest will endure a little longer, into November (and a few will greet the new year), but tomorrow, or next week, another gale will whip most of them away. While they last, their beauty distracts the mind. Indoors, one feels guilty at not being out of doors. Out of doors, one is blinded by the pageant. But whether inside or out, one overhears the triumphant voice of Emily Bronte:

> Fall, leaves, fall; die, flowers, away;
> Lengthen night and shorten day:
> Every leaf speaks bliss to me
> Fluttering from an autumn tree;
> I shall smile when wreaths of snow
> Blossom where the rose should grow;
> I shall sing when night's decay
> Ushers in the drearier day.

I take pleasure from knowing that I am not the only man who makes an April Fool of himself twelve times a year and once a month. In January, when the evening star floats on the water, I say, "The year has nothing to excel this." In February, saluting the first snowdrop, I make the same assertion, which, with equal confidence, I repeat to the winds of March because, with April, they bring forth the May flowers. And so throughout the seasons: what I shall say of the snow in December I say now in October of these leaves on the water and of those others that have yet to fall: "The year has nothing to excel this."

XI

DARK BLUE WATERS: RADLEY TO EYNSHAM

THE Thames leaves Abingdon proudly, both for what it has received and for what it is about to be given—the wooded parkland of Nuneham Courtenay, which descends to the Oxford bank, marred briefly by modernity's Black Bridge (known sometimes as the Ebony Bastard).

Beyond the bridge an island appears, marking the site of a former lock and its keeper's thatched cottage.

In 1710 the Lord High Chancellor of England, Viscount Harcourt, relinquished his ancestral seat at Stanton Harcourt, twenty miles up-river, and bought the manor house at Nuneham Courtenay, which had belonged since 1214 to the Courtenays. The house was a small one, and after half a century the Harcourts replaced it by the present mansion, designed by Leadbetter, architect of Oxford's Radcliffe Infirmary, who used a quantity of stones from the old house at Stanton Harcourt.

The estate covers some 1,600 acres, most of it laid-out by "Capability" Brown, who was born at Kirkharle in Northumberland, where you may still see traces of the landscape which he planned for the lord of that manor. Claud and Poussin would look well among these gardens, or wandering through the deer park. There is a stone folly here, called Carfax. It was part of a conduit that was removed from Oxford's Carfax in order to make room for eighteenth-century traffic. Here also is Whitehead's Oak, commemorating the poet.

William Whitehead—he received the Laureateship solely because Gray had declined it—was born in 1715, the son of a Cambridge baker. Having taken a scholarship to Winchester and thence (since New College would not have him) a sizarship at Clare Hall, Whitehead spent his time amassing poor poetry and rich connections; from which latter he extracted a by-product of sons with whom he undertook the Grand Tour of Europe. That is how he came to know the Harcourts. In a piece called *The Danger of Writing Verse* Whitehead asks:

> Say, can the bard attempt what's truly great,
> Who pants in secret for his future fate?

Shakespeare, one feels, panted a great deal while writing *King Lear*; and Milton came very close to demanding the "Heav'nly Muse's" immortality before he had written six lines in pursuit of it. Whitehead himself composed an average of two official odes per annum. Before he became Poet Laureate he wrote a piece to mark the birth of Frederick, later Prince of Wales.

> Thanks, Nature, thanks; the finish'd piece we own,
> And worthy Fred'ric's love, and Britain's throne.
> Th' impatient goddess first and sketched the plan,
> Yet, ere she durst compleat the wondrous man,
> To try her power a gentler task design'd,
> And form'd a pattern of a softer kind.

The "pattern of a softer kind" was the Lady Augusta. Whitehead died at Charles Street, Grosvenor Square, in 1785; and Coventry Patmore wrote a preface for his collected poems.

Nuneham Courtenay has two churches: the former parish church (which became the Harcourt chapel) and the present parish church (which the Harcourts built in 1880, for the greater convenience of the villagers).

The village itself has literally moved with the times, for the Harcourts not only demolished the manor house but also removed the village, giving its dispossessed persons a new home on the main road to Oxford. One assumes that for most of them it seemed a good thing; instead of communing with the Thames, they gossiped with the coachmen.

Nuneham Courtenay was still a new village when Pastor Moritz sampled its hospitality. He has walked from Nettlebed, a few miles above Henley-on-Thames, which he found "the perfect village". Now it is night, and he feels tired. The inn at Nuneham tells him that it has no room (which may be true), and when he asks for food: "The only answer I got was that since I wouldn't be spending the night there it wouldn't be fair for them to feed me. I could go my way and sup where I slept. Then I demanded a pot of beer, which they deigned to give me for ready money, but a slice of bread—for which I would gladly have paid in cash—they refused. Such astonishing inhospitality I hadn't expected, even at an English inn."

Innkeepers seem to have mended their ways during the half-century between Moritz's experience of English inns and Dickens's description of them. But the Pastor travelled on foot, and such people were regarded as potential brigands. Not until the nineteenth century did hikers become respectable, though hike is an old English word which grew obsolete and then returned from America during the 1920s. Modern travellers along the Thames sometimes receive the same sort of inhospitality that was offered to Pastor Moritz in 1782. A word on that subject, therefore, may prove helpful. The Law does not regard an inn as being necessarily the same as a tavern, alehouse, or pub (which are not compelled to serve customers). But an innkeeper—that is, the keeper of a place providing accommodation for travellers—must supply lodging and refreshment, at any hour of the day or night, to anyone who conducts himself decently and is able to pay for services. Thieves, prostitutes, and persons suffering from a contagious illness may be turned away.

The river, meanwhile, has been backing from north to north-west, still accompanied by the woods of Nuneham Park. Presently the woods cease, at a point where a ferry serves Radley.

There are two Radleys, Upper and Lower. The former has become a suburb of Oxford, and that is that. Its fifteenth-century church introduces yet another Speaker of the House of Commons, for the canopy above the pulpit was taken from the old House of Commons by Mr. Speaker Lenthall, who in 1653 presented it to Radley. Here, too, is some medieval glass, showing the arms of Kings Richard III, Henry VI, and Henry VIII, alongside some good modern glass (but no one has yet recaptured the warmth of that medieval red).

Lower Radley still has some thatched cottages, but no amount of architecture can of itself create village life; and in that fact one confronts another difference between the Thames as it was and as it has become. From time immemorial the villagers looked for leadership, and found it in the parson and in the lord of the manor. Those leaders were always fallible, often inept, sometimes evil; but they did knit a collection of individuals into a corporate entity. Nowadays, by contrast, the average English village has become leaderless. No semi-residential businessman, no Women's Institute—least of all Whitehall—can replace the parson and the squire. Not even the parish council can replace them. This may be regrettable, for a variety of reasons; but it remains a fact. An experienced traveller can usually decide, after a few minutes' exploration, whether a village is leaderless or whether it still retains its shepherd.

Radley College, standing beyond the church, began as Radley House in 1727—a brick building with Victorian additions. The school was founded by Dr. Sewell in 1847, and enjoys a fine rowing reputation. It first competed at Henley in 1861, when it went down to Eton; but in 1877 the Henley Stewards arranged a special race between Radley and Cheltenham, which Radley won. In 1952 the College took both the Princess Elizabeth Cup and the record time. And on that note, as the College boat house appears, the river enters dark blue water.

I find it difficult to define the change which comes over the Thames as it approaches Oxford. It is not so much a metamorphosis, a drastic change of appearance, as a modification of specific features. At Teddington, for example, the Thames seemed to be public property (people walked by it, sculled on it, drove past it), and at Medmenham it seemed to be private property (which you shared with a few guests). But at Radley the Thames seems neither private nor public. Even on a fine Sunday the towing path looks empty, which is strange because the city of dreaming spires used to be a city of striding legs.

Between Radley and Eynsham the Thames has witnessed famous feats of walkmanship. In the 1920s Dr. Phelps, Provost of Oriel, invited undergraduates to take tea with him, having walked them so far and so fast that several fell by the way. A Brasenose man, John Buchan, first Lord Tweedsmuir, once walked sixty-three miles in a single day; and when, in later life, he made his home near this reach, he walked a weekly circuit of Otmoor, some thirty miles or more. Edward Thomas of Lincoln College wrote several essays about walking and boating: his widow said: ". . . of all his pleasures, walking was the deepest and most comprehensive". Thomas de Quincey of Worcester College walked through a great part of England, and even as an elderly man covered his daily stint of between eight and fifteen miles. In the

1890s Hilaire Belloc of Balliol walked the fifty-two miles from Oxford to Marble Arch in a little over eleven hours. Sixty years later three Oxford undergraduates tried to break Belloc's record, and failed. Belloc was a boating man, too. Between sunrise and sunset of a short winter day he paddled his canoe along forty miles of winding river. From Saint Mary's Church in Oxford to Saint Mary's Church in Cambridge, a distance of eighty miles, was a favourite week-end stroll.

From Radley meanwhile the Thames has travelled a mile or so to Sandford Lock, dominated by a paper mill. On the Berkshire bank a lashing weir invites a wide berth, though people still bathe there despite the memorial to a couple of Christchurch under-graduates who were swept away and drowned. Sandford-on-Thames is of no interest unless for an old farmhouse on the site of a thirteenth-century preceptory of the Templars. A doorway and some windows of the Preceptory have been incorporated in the house and farm buildings.

Now Kennington Island appears, and with it the first tinge of industrial Oxford. The French King knew that he would escape the deluge; ours is unavoidable; and before it does strike, some travellers will wish to make a short pilgrimage from Kennington into Littlemore, where Cardinal Newman lived.

When John Henry Newman at last went over to Rome, he was shabbily treated by it, through the jealousy of a fellow-convert, Cardinal Manning, whose secretary, Monsignor George Talbot, warned him: "Dr. Newman is more English than the English. His spirit must be crushed." Not even Rome could do that, and Newman in his age was made a Cardinal.

But Newman's link with Littlemore had been forged long before his conversion, for he was a Fellow of Oriel and vicar of the University church of Saint Mary. In 1836 he built at Littlemore a chapel-of-ease, hoping to expand it into a religious retreat. Five years later he published the famous ninetieth of his Tracts, which put a Romanized interpretation on the Thirty Nine Articles. At that time he was still trying to accomplish what Wesley had failed to achieve—a renascence within the Establishment. But Tract 90 made his conversion inevitable. He set Saint Mary's in the care of a curate, and retreated to Littlemore, taking with him from Oriel his library of books. It is nowadays difficult to believe that the welfare of the Church of England, and the renascence within the Church of Rome, were once regarded by the majority of educated Englishmen as matters of grave importance. At Littlemore the Press pursued the man who, they feared, would betray Anglicanism. "I cannot walk into or out of my house," Newman complained, "but curious eyes are upon me. I had thought that an Englishman's house was his castle, but the newspapers thought otherwise. . . ."

On 8th October, 1845, in his house at Littlemore, at about six o'clock in the evening, during a storm, Newman was received into the Roman Church, with two other Anglican priests, by a Passionist, Father Dominic, whom he described as "a simple, holy man; and withal gifted with remarkable powers".

Newman's one worldly ambition had been to live and work and die in the University of Oxford, but on his submission he left that city, and entered it only once again, after an absence of thirty years. In his *Apologia*, that sublimity of prose, Newman concluded the account of his spiritual Damascus with some lines of loving remembrance—not, indeed, of Oriel, where he was troubled, but towards Trinity, where he had graduated. "There used," he wrote, "to be much snap-dragon growing on the walls of my freshman's rooms there, and I had for years taken it as an emblem of my perpetual residence even unto death in my university." As he walked beside the Thames, this saintly man, whom Kingsley had arraigned as a cheat, must have composed in his mind many of the great fugues which at Littlemore he set down in the other harmony of prose; among them his beautiful nightpiece: "O Lord, support us all the day long in this troublous life, until the shadows lengthen, and the evening comes, and the busy world is hushed, and the fever of life is over, and our work is done. Then, Lord, in thy mercy, grant us safe lodging, a holy rest, and peace at the last."

Newman's village is buried beneath a wilderness of villas, but Oriel still holds the advowson of the church he built there, and in 1967 its vicar was himself an Oriel man, Reverend Valentine Fletcher.

Iffley stands a short way above Kennington Island, and has become a suburb of Morrisland; its twelfth-century church is justly famous, looking much the same as when it was built . . . the Norman nave, the doorways carved with fishes and animals and birds, the massive font and its bowl of black marble.

Iffley water-mill was destroyed by fire in 1908, but a part of it escaped and is now a tea-house, Grist Cottage, overlooking the leet.

By and large, the entry into Oxford is marvellously unspoiled. The river suddenly narrows, and develops an acute bend (or Gut) so that the uninitiate, arriving during Torpids or in Eights Week, may fancy they overhead someone saying, "Last night Teddy Hall was bumped in the guts" (which means, the St. Edmund Hall crew was at that point more than overtaken by its immediate pursuer).

Christchurch Meadows, on the right bank, flaunt many fine trees. Here Samuel Johnson of Pembroke College cut a lecture in order to skate on the frozen floods. The lecturer justified his name of Meeke: "I once had a whole morning sliding in Christ Church meadows," Johnson told Boswell, "and missed his lecture in logick. After dinner he sent for me to his room. I expected a sharp rebuke for my idleness, and went with a beating heart. When we were seated, he told me had sent for me to drink a glass of wine with him, and to tell me, he was *not* angry with me for missing his lecture. This was, in fact, a most severe reprimand."

On this reach the College barges are moored. Originally they were brought from City livery companies, as grandstands from which to watch the racing. In time they were replaced by replicas or by newer barges; but one of the original City barges remains —it belongs to Oriel—with a Viking prow, elliptical windows, angelic carvings.

This indeed is the darkest reach of blue waters, and on it was born the dexterity of eight-oared rowing. In 1807 Robert Southey of Balliol wrote: ". . . a number of pleasure boats were gliding in all directions upon this clear and rapid stream; some with spread sails, in others caps and tassels of the students formed a curious contrast with their employment at the oar." The first bumping races took place in 1815, with Brasenose going Head of the River, followed by Jesus (but since these seem to have been the only entrants, they may be described as having been at the top of their form in a class by themselves). Christ Church soon joined in (wearing vivid tam-o'-shanters) and by 1824 Exeter had arrived (with a boat from Plymouth Dockyard). Next came Balliol, Worcester, Trinity. Andrew Lang, Fellow of Merton, declared ". . . boating men are the salt of the University, so steady, so well disciplined, so good-tempered. . . ." On this reach, even today, all lesser craft give way before the elected gods, as Charles Kingsley noticed long ago: ". . . the University Eight, with little blue flag at her bows, went rushing down the river on her splendid course." For a musical portrait of this reach one may turn to another great river, the Danube, from whose basin flowed the roistering aristocrats evoked by the Swedish composer's *The Entry of the Boyars.*

Then, within sight of Folly Bridge, all passion is spent, all beauty dissolved, decency itself violated by Mammon's inhumanity to man. This state of affairs is relatively modern, for when Pastor Moritz had failed to buy a crust of bread at Nuneham Courtenay 200 years ago, he fell in with a don who, like himself, was making for Oxford; and as they came within sight of that city, the don said to the pastor: "You will soon see one of the most beautiful and superb cities, not merely in England but in all Europe." That city has disappeared, leaving behind a nucleus of colleges, deafened by the electrons of traffic.

Windsor, we agreed, was a portrait in itself; and so were Hampton Court and Abingdon; but the University of Oxford is more than a portrait—it is a gallery of portraits. To the traveller who disembarks here I can do no more than commend three times of arrival.

First: on a May morning, when sunlight and a blue sky add edge to the curving High; before the traffic has arrived, but in time to see the city sprinkled with a policeman, one or two undergraduates who have arisen early in order to keep themselves trim, and an old don who has arisen early because he has been doing so every morning since he went up sixty years ago.

Second: in early October, during the vacation, when college walls are ablaze with creeper, and no frost has yet dimmed the flowers. Wander through Saint John's and beside the lake at Worcester, or squeeze yourself into the intimacy of Saint Edmund Hall. Then, despite the traffic, you will find what Charles Lamb found—he who, as he put it, "had been defrauded in his young years of the sweet food of academic institution", yet could say without bitterness—"The walks at these times are so much one's own—the tall trees of Christ's, the groves of Magdalen. The halls deserted, and with open doors, inviting one to slip in unperceived, and pay a devoir to some Founder. . . ."

Last: late on a snowy night, when the flakes curtsey to the cobbles of Merton Street, past lamp-lit windows where a type-writer taps, or good humour laughs, or Bach speaks the Esperanto of his native tongue. Then, as Great Tom prepares to unleash its midnight carillon, turn into Oriel Street, under the shadow of the college where the ghosts of Sir Thomas More and of Sir Walter Raleigh mingle with the memories of kings, poets, prelates, peers, and the vast body of unknown men who in their day gave thanks that they too were once of so great a company.

Do these things at these times, and you will receive the best of what Oxford has to bestow. But at almost any other season you will find yourself in what might be one of half-a-hundred over-blown, shop-streaked, car-crammed, loud-mouthed, hygienically unhealthy hives.

As for Folly Bridge, it records an interesting story. The Norman bridge had eighteen arches and a towered gatehouse marking the ford where oxen crossed the Thames. In that tower dwelt Friar Bacon, who was England's Leonardo da Vinci, a type of universal genius.

Roger Bacon was born near Ilchester in or about the year 1210. Having studied at Oxford, he followed the fashion by reading in Paris. In a non-specialized age he was content to master physics, astronomy, philosophy, logic, literature, theology, grammar, history. Pope Clement II commissioned him to write down everything that was known about anything; which he did. Of his sixteen major works, all in Latin, I am innocent, but I do happen to have browsed through a sixteenth-century book called *The Famous Historie of Fryer Bacon*, parts of which offer a verbatim paraphrase of the volumes he compiled in his study on Folly Bridge. "Chariots shall move," he prophesied, "with an un-speakable force, without any living creature to stirre them." Likewise, he added, "an instrument may be made to fly withall. . . . By art also an instrument may be made, where with men may walk in the bottom of the sea or rivers. . . . Also, perspects may be so framed that things farre off shall seem nigh unto us." Whether this Franciscan did invent gunpowder is debatable; that he kept abreast of the future is proven. Truly one may say of this Oxonian what Vasari remarked of Leonardo da Vinci: "In the normal course of events many men and women are born with remarkable qualities and talents; but occasionally, in a way that transcends nature, a single person is marvellously endowed . . . in such abundance that he leaves other men far behind. . . ."

Long after Bacon's death, his tower received an extra storey—whence the name Folly—but was demolished at the end of the eighteenth century. The present bridge was built in or about 1826.

Above Folly Bridge the river is joined by a stream which soon afterwards goes underground. An Oxford schoolboy once canoed through this Lethe-like waterway. Later, having graduated at Magdalen, he became a soldier, attained the rank of Lieutenant Colonel, then of Aircraftman, and is today known as Lawrence of Arabia.

For the next mile the river skulks through a smelly, smokey, gas-worked, rail-ridden, house-heaped desolation of abominable prosperity: Reading, in short, writ small. Right and left is a maze of rivulets and canals: on the left bank the Seacourt Stream, the Hinksey Stream, and a quadrangle of water-ways around Osney; on the right bank a double-fork into the Oxford Canal. Here we confront the ghost of James Brindley again, for a meeting of the Oxford Canal Navigation—held at the "Three Tuns", Banbury, in 1790—chose him to be their chief engineer. At the beginning of the twentieth century Brindley's Oxford Canal was carrying some 450,000 tons of goods a year. Even today it plies a modest trade in coal. During its hey-day it carried barges to the Warwick and Napton Canal, to the Grand Junction Canal, to the Coventry Canal.

Although it fought a losing battle, the University of Oxford did succeed in keeping the railway at a decent distance. Brunel's Great Western arrived first, with a line from Didcot to Folly Bridge. That was in 1844. The first trains from London to Oxford took six hours—an average speed of about eight miles an hour. In 1852 Oxford became an important junction, with a line to Worcester (1852) and another to Thame (1863). But the opposition had already arrived in 1851, with a line to Bletchley and thence to Cambridge.

As though to discourage traffic, Osney's nineteenth-century bridge makes even a short man crouch when he passes beneath it—only seven feet and six inches above the water.

Osney Abbey has disappeared, but not wholly without trace, for its medieval bell, Great Tom (or Old Tom) was hung in

Wren's tower at Christ Church. This bell was recast in or about the year 1680. It weighs seven tons, and has a girth of seven yards. Every night at five-past-nine it sounds a curfew, striking one hundred and one times, that being the number of undergraduates in Wolsey's Cardinal College. At the sound, when I was an undergraduate, every college closed its gates, and if we wished to remain out of college after that time, we had to obtain permission. Tom, by the way, became a favourite name for medieval bells, and not by chance; it was England's tribute to the foremost of her martyrs, St. Thomas Becket.

In 1754, when Dr. Johnson revisited Oxford, he and Boswell came walking this way. "Once," Boswell remembered, "in our way home, we viewed the ruins of the abbies of Oseney and Rewley, near Oxford." Indignant that such buildings should have been allowed to crumble, Johnson lapsed into an unwonted dumbness: "After at least half an hour's silence," Johnson said, 'I viewed them with indignation'."

Now on the right Port Meadow appears, 400 acres of grazing land that has belonged to the Oxford freemen since the reign of Edward the Confessor. Even today it is common ground for cattle, sheep, horses, goats, geese, dogs, cats, lovers and old men reading cantankerous newspapers.

Presently things start to look up. Indeed, the worst of Oxford fell astern at Fiddler's Island, facing Medley Manor. Three centuries ago George Withers wrote:

> In summetime to Medley
> My love and I would go.

One wonders whether Housman had read and unconsciously copied that couplet:

> In summertime on Bredon
> . . . My love and I would lie.

Facing Port Meadow, Binsey recalls another poet, Gerard Manley Hopkins, who witnessed the first beginnings of the ruin of Oxford.

Hopkins went up to Balliol in 1863, where he became a good botanist and a tireless walker. At Binsey he especially admired a row of poplars—"my aspens dear"—and continued to visit them for several years; but in 1874, returning after a long absence, he found that the poplars had disappeared. The loss cut the lonely Jesuit's heart:

> Ten or twelve only ten or twelve
> Strokes of havoc unselve
> The sweet especial scene
> The rural scene, a rural scene,
> Sweet especial rural scene.

But Hopkins had lost something more than a rural scene. The city and university of Oxford were slipping away, filched by the builders, year after year consumed with cancer: "a graceless growth," Hopkins called it, "base and brickish."

Binsey is indeed encircled by base bricks. If you arrive by water, you may pass the village without seeing it; if you come by land, you must brave the horrors of the Botley road with its hideous cinema, unsightly shops, ugly traffic. Yet when I first saw Binsey (the ancient *Beneseye* or "Byni's Island") I found there a pub, a farm, a church, a cluster of cottages—marooned among watermeadows. Today they have built factories and yards along the lane where cows once went, swaying slowly, to sip the Thames. Even so, the Norman church abides in glorious isolation, at the end of an avenue of chestnut trees, along a lane raised against floods. On my first visit the church was lit by oil lamps.

Here, they say, St. Frideswide discovered a miraculous stream of water. Frideswide was born towards the end of the eighth century, daughter of an Ealdorman named Dida. When another nobleman, Algar, asked for her hand in marriage, she refused, preferring the religious life. She founded, and became first abbess of, the Oxford nunnery of St. Mary; and at Binsey she built a small chapel, which became a place of pilgrimage and of money-makers who cornered the market in miraculous water. One may disbelieve 99 per cent of the alleged cures at saintly shrines, but the undoubted 1 per cent remains, for water is a strange thing. If he can bring himself to believe in its healing properties, even a Behaviourist may be cured of psycho-somaticism by swallowing a spoonful of puddle.

Now Godstow Lock is in sight, offering a last vision of Oxford, as Hopkins saw it:

> Towered city and branchy between towers.

Cotswold country: in Bampton

And between branches those towers fall from sight, though never out of mind. The greatest of Oxford's breed have praised her with the passion of a lover, have loved her with the loyalty of a son, have served her with the duty of a knight; and their tribute is the more eloquent because it comes from every corner of the kingdom, from men who owe allegiance to the mountains, or to the marshland, or to the sea that encircles them. Wordsworth himself, a Cambridge man, was moved to cry:

> O ye spires of Oxford! domes and towers!
> Gardens and groves! Your presence overpowers. . . .

Matthew Arnold, that thorn in the heart of the Philistines, praised her with an irony almost too delicate to be detected: ". . . home of lost causes, and forsaken beliefs, and unpopular names, and impossible loyalties." Quiller-Couch, who came here from Cornwall, praised her through the lips of another youth from another region: "So this was Oxford; more beautiful than all his dreams!" Much of that beauty has been marred beyond mending, and the residue resembles a precious stone set among pastework; but within that precious stone a perdurable quality abides, of which Robert Bridges prophesied:

> Time shall against himself thy house uphold.

This reach of the river invites a question: what was the most memorable voyage ever made upon the Thames? The question will sound less idle if "memorable" is taken to mean the longest remembrance, for the worthiest reasons, by the greatest number of people. My own answer is—the voyage to Godstow that was made during the afternoon of 4th July, 1862, by three small girls (their average age being ten years) and a couple of middle-aged men; Robin Duckworth, who afterwards became Dean of Westminster, and a friend of his.

As the skiff glided up-stream the friend, who was rowing bow, began to tell rather an amusing tale to the child who steered. The tale, as the Dean recalled, "was told over my shoulder . . . I remember turning round and saying, 'Is this an extempore romance of yours?' And he replied, 'Yes, I'm inventing it as we go along.' " The storyteller, as it happened, managed to remember his tale, and later wrote it down. It opens as follows: "Alice was beginning to get very tired of sitting by her sisters on the bank,

10

Norman porch, St. Samson's Church, Cricklade

and of having nothing to do. . . ." So was born *Alice in Wonderland*, of whom it may be said that she arose like Venus from the water.

Her creator—a Cheshire man, Charles Lutwidge Dodgson—was a deacon who felt too shy ever to become a priest, and contented himself by teaching mathematics at Christ Church. Dodgson stammered, had a tilted shoulder, never married, and favoured the company of little girls. Inevitably he became the subject of psycho-analytic monographs, some of which are absurd, and even the best a stumbling block to the uninhibited enjoyment of his fantasy. One may accept a large part of the Freudian credo, yet still believe that to analyse *Alice In Wonderland* is akin to summoning the Fire Brigade in order to ascertain its opinion of Niagara Falls. Like Hans Andersen, Dodgson was an innocent who would have been appalled had he understood the dynamics of his "respectable" fondness for little girls. What a pity, by the way, that there is no truth in the story that Queen Victoria, enchanted by *Alice In Wonderland*, asked that the Oxford mathematician's next book be dedicated to herself; which of course it was, entitled *Condensation Of Determinants*.

Dodgson's Thames-born classic was not launched without mishap. When only forty-eight copies of the first edition had been sold or given away, its illustrator, Tenniel, protested against the quality of the reproduction of his drawings. The edition was therefore withdrawn, and its unbound sheets sold to America. A manuscript copy of that edition went to the British Museum for £15,400, but the manuscript from which the compositor set up the first edition has never been found.

Fortunately, Alice recovered. The book has been filmed and dramatized; its illustrations have been used as wallpaper; it has been translated into twenty-four languages and two shorthand versions; and in 1911 it was banned by the Province of Huan, on the ground that animals which could speak were an insult to the dignity of man.

It was in order to escape from this publicity that Dodgson devised a pen-name, Lewis Carroll—a play on Lutwidge (or Lewis) and Charles (or Carolus). The device failed. One morning Dodson awoke and found that he was famous. The prime minister, Sir Robert Peel, offered him preferment; the Oxford postal service wilted under the weight of correspondence (some of it was addressed to Alice, Oxford); and when Dodson died, a thirteen-year-old girl wrote to the *Saint James's Gazette*, suggesting that a memorial fund might "collect money to have a cot in the Children's Hospital, and call it the Alice In Wonderland cot". This appeal was answered by the Royal Family and by many eminent artists—Rossetti, Meredith, Blackmore, Holman Hunt, Irving, Madge Kendal, and the man who wrote another Thames classic, Jerome K. Jerome.

So, back once more to the river and to the lines in which Lewis Carroll told how Alice was born:

> All in a golden afternoon
> Full leisurely we glide . . .
> Thus grew the tale of Wonderland:
> Thus slowly, one by one,
> Its quaint events were hammered out—
> And now the tale is done.

But not quite: the afternoon was not "golden". Records in the London Meteorological Office prove that on 4th July, 1862, the weather at Godstow was "cool and rather wet". *N'importe*, for Alice still creates her own sunnyland.

Suddenly the Thames becomes medieval: a statement so vague and of such evident impossibility that it must be defended, or at any rate more closely defined. Now, the Tower of London was medieval, and Windsor Castle was medieval, and continuously since Teddington the river has passed medieval sites and medieval memories; yet the traveller did not feel as though he were voyaging into the past. Such of the past as he did notice was predominantly Tudor, or Georgian, or Victorian; and all of it was out-dated by the present. But at Godstow—unless I am utterly the victim of self-mesmerism—that state of affairs ceases and is replaced by at least a possibility that Duns Scotus will appear, or William of Occam, so profoundly meditating a point of logic that only by a razorbreadth do they avoid walking into the river. Two facts emphasize the point (or "whimsy" as Defoe called such impressions). The first fact is, you can walk all day from Godstow at four miles an hour without passing through a village or a town. The second fact is Godstow Nunnery—"the house," as Stow described it, "of Nunes beside Oxford"—whose fragmentary ruins overlook the river.

Godstow Nunnery was consecrated in the presence of King

Stephen and of its founder, Didan, who had raised it for his daughter, Frideswide—she having emerged from the comparative safety of Bampton-in-the-Bush, a dozen miles up-river, where she eluded the unsolicited attentions of Algar. Saintliness, however never has managed to seem quite so popular as sex, and Godstow is known rather on account of Rosamund than by reason of Frideswide.

Fair Rosamund (as she came to be called) was of the noble house of Clifford, and may have been a pupil at Godstow Convent. Henry III noticed her, and installed her as his mistress at Woodstock. There is no evidence to confirm the legend that the Queen tracked the mistress to a secret lair, and then invited her to choose either a dagger or a cup of poison; nor is there any reason to believe that the King caused a tunnel to be built between Godstow and Woodstock (it would have demanded many hours' crawling).

The truth is, the Lady Rosamund soon ceased to seem novel. So, she retired to Godstow Nunnery, a somewhat experienced novice, and died there in 1176. Fifteen years later Bishop Hugh of Lincoln discovered that her tomb was still lit by candles and lamps, and adorned with tapestry. The Saint thereupon called the sinner a harlot, and ordered that the body be removed. By the sixteenth century Leland was able to report that even the tomb had disappeared: "Rosamund's tomb at Godstow was taken up of late."

After the Dissolution, Godstow Nunnery became a private residence, which Lord Fairfax razed in 1646, leaving only a doorway and fragments of the wall. Today it is as it was in 1810, when Thomas Love Peacock wrote:

> The wind-flower waves, in lonely bloom,
> On Godstow's desolated wall.

On the opposite bank the popular Trout Inn—like the less publicized Perch Inn at Binsey—confirms a piscatorial reach. Generations of undergraduates have passed this way, for the Trout Inn possesses some handsome peacocks, and is altogether an impressive rendezvous.

A backwater from the Trout Inn makes a detour that rejoins the river at King's Lock, one mile further on. During its detour the stream passes Wolvercote, which is not handsome, but does contain a paper-mill serving the Oxford University Press.

The first Oxford book was printed in 1468 (or 1478: a misprint has confused the matter) by a Cologne man, Theodoric Rood. It was a commentary on the Apostles' Creed, allegedly by St. Jerome. In 1584 the Chancellor of the University, Robert Dudley, Earl of Leicester, suggested that Convocation launch a printing press of its own, which it did, the next year, by lending £100 to an Oxford bookseller, Joseph Barnes, who printed *inter alia* the first Oxford book in Hebrew and the first in Greek. This new-found Oxford University Press was licensed to print Bibles. Had it foreseen how literately pious the world was soon to become, it would never have sold its licence to the Stationers' Company for a couple of quid. In 1665, when the King was at Oxford, the University Press published England's first newspaper, *The Oxford Gazette*.

Wolvercote Mill was established three centuries ago by Dr. John Fell, Chaplain to the King, Dean of Christ Church, Bishop of Oxford; whose name has been scurrilously bandied down ever since Thomas Brown wrote:

> I do not love thee, Dr. Fell,
> The reason why I cannot tell;
> But this alone I know full well,
> I do not love thee, Dr. Fell.

When Brown said that he did not know why he disliked Dr. Fell, he was lying. He knew very well indeed, having composed his jingle *ex tempore* when the Doctor threatened to send him down for misconduct. A contemporary said of Dr. Fell, that he was "most pedantic and pedagogical, yet still aimed at the public good". Certainly he spent much of his own money on the Press, and persuaded Archbishop Sheldon to house it in the Sheldonian Theatre. Even better, he managed to regain from the Stationers' Company the right to print Bibles and Prayer Books (whence the Press's Amen House in appropriate Paternoster Row). Between 1702 and 1704 the Oxford University Press printed a three-volume edition of Lord Clarendon's *The True Historical Narrative of the Rebellion and the Civil Wars in England*, which sold so well that the publishers commissioned Sir John Vanburgh to design the Clarendon Printing House. Today the imprint of the Oxford University Press is coveted alike by scholars and poets throughout the world.

This reach of the river, too, has its own imprint or signature tune, composed by an unknown monk who on a day in spring went walking beside the Thames, where he saw that the sky was blue, heard that the lambs were gay, smelled that the grass was green, and altogether paid proper attention to primroses, fledglings, and new-born leaves. And having done those things, he went one better and made of them a song which, though it is seven centuries old, sparkles so freshly that one might suppose it to have come new-minted from the lips of a man who had never heard of Contemporary Verse:

> Summer is icumen in,
> Loud sing cuckoo!
> Groweth seed, and bloweth mead,
> And springeth the wood anew—
> Sing cuckoo!

Walking this way one November morning I found myself accompanied by a fellow-traveller whose presence was audible though motionless—the chatter of reeds with a wind. Sometimes the sound was quite startling, like rattling bones. It was then that I learned how swiftly the Thames will change its countenance. Within the space of two minutes the surface switched from blue to grey, from grey to silver, from silver to lead; all in rhythm with sunlight and scudding clouds. Here I have met men for whom the reeds once meant more than a companionable sound, for they lit life after dark, and were known as rushlights. In 1880, at a time when trains were racing to Scotland at seventy miles an hour, a yearbook recorded that "the antiquated rushlight is still an article of domestic use. Messrs. Haynes supply between three and four tons annually . . ." (the surprise is in the tail) ". . . chiefly to the Universities".

Gilbert White, being Vice-Provost of Oriel and a great walker, must often have passed this way. He certainly left a scholarly account of how rushlights were made: "The proper species of rushlight for this purpose seems to be the common soft rush found in most pastures. They are in the best condition at the height of summer." Each reed was so peeled as to leave a narrow rib supporting the pith. After that, the reeds were bleached, dried, and dipped in boiling fat. 1,600 reeds weighed one pound, and needed six pounds of grease. Gilbert White was precise: "A good rush which measured in length two feet four inches and a half . . . burned only three minutes short of an hour." Such reeds, he reported, "give a good clear light". Less than twenty pounds of fat, he added, sufficed one family for a twelvemonth ". . . since working people burn no candles in the long days, because they rise and go to bed by day-light." Eleven rushes, giving light for twelve hours, cost one farthing.

Rushes abound near King's Lock where the river turns sharp left past Oxey Mead. Pixey Mead, and West Mead, which record a brand of "liquid history" not less memorable than Windsor Castle, though few have heard of it. Here, each July, the riverside meadows are drawn by lot: Oxey Mead first, then West Mead, finally Pixey Mead. And this is done as follows: thirteen balls of cherry wood are kept at Mead Farm, each painted with a name. Many famous names have been heard *en route*; let us now praise the less famous names of the men who owned shares in these Meads . . . Freeman, Rothe, Green, William of Bladon, Waterey Molly, Gilbert, Geoffrey, Dunn, White, Parry, Harry, Boulton, Boat. Two elected Meadsmen walk to a strip of each meadow, and a disinterested person is asked to pick a ball from the bag, and read its name. The owner of the ball which bears that name then comes forward to take possession of his strip for the ensuing year, which he does by mowing a small segment of it, and cutting his initials in the grass. Today a main road slashes part of the Meads but the medieval custom survives.

West Mead is sometimes known as Yarnton Mead, after the village a little way inland. This is Spencer-Churchill country, for the manor-house was built in 1612 by Sir Thomas Spencer whose arms adorn the entrance, and not simply as an ornament—they are pierced with peep-holes for musketeers. This same Sir Thomas restored the tower of the Norman church, and in it built his family chapel, shielded by railings containing a monument to a Victorian Duchess of Marlborough. Less exalted was William Fletcher, a villager who died in 1826, and is remembered by a brass.

Now the Thames steers south-west towards Wytham Great Wood, inland on the left, seeming both high and mighty above the level meadows. In October you may notice the influence of altitude on this wood; the lower trees retain their leaves for at least a week longer than trees on the windswept summit.

Here the Evenlode chimes in, among so many curves that a walker feels tempted to cut across the fields, but the temptation must be resisted because many of these fields carry barbed wire too high to be leaped, too low to be wriggled. In any event, there seems no hurry, and the going is good indeed, for presently Wytham Great Wood comes down to the river, and in places sends out an avenue above the towing-path, very welcome when rain has squelched the land within a hundred yards of the water. No matter how strong your fondness for Cliveden, nor how loyal your allegiance to the Chilterns, here, you feel, is a country that will go on deepening until journey's end. And although at this point the river offers no stately home, it does have a tale to tell.

On Saturday, 27th July, 1588, a vessel set out from Mousehole, near Penzance, with a cargo of salt for France. Between Ushant and the Scillies she sighted nine great ships bearing north-east towards England, their sails slashed with scarlet crosses. The Cornish skipper needed no one to tell him that he had sighted part of Philips's enterprise, the Great Armada. Valorously discreet, he put about and made for Mousehole; but the Spaniards sighted him and sent their fastest ships to sink him. Fortunately for England, the Cornishman escaped and brought the news home to Penzance. The member of Parliament for Cornwall, Sir Sidney Godolphin, at once sent a courier to inform the Lord High Admiral, Lord Howard of Effingham, a better Englishman than he was a Roman Catholic. In due course the beacons blazed, warning the kingdom of its peril. Eastward like answering lamps they lit the night, causing who knows what consternation among the villagers as they looked up and saw that old Tom or young Jack, so far from sleeping at their post, had seen the western sky, and were now piling the faggots on their own English candle. And among such folk were the villagers of Eynsham when they saw that Beacon Hill, overlooking the Thames, had leaped alive, out of the flames that baptized it.

Eynsham lies a mile or so north of the river. Swinford Bridge is one of the two remaining toll bridges on the Thames, built by Lord Abingdon in 1777. Until recently the toll was one penny per wheel. Now, like the cost of living, it has ascended even nearer to the price that passeth understanding. The toll-house is not perceptibly improved by its television aerial. A few yards away stands a modern power-house, designed in the eighteenth-century manner, as though to emphasize that the eighteenth century never did design a modern power-house. Even so, the anachronism is less obtrusive than the modern manner.

Until recent time Eynsham was a village; now it is a suburb of Oxford. It has a cross in the market place, twenty feet tall, the lantern head rising from a slender shaft. Aelfric was Abbot of Eynsham; that learned man from Abingdon, who had been Abbot of Winchester and then of Cerne. He studied under Aethelwold, and composed two books of *Homilies* setting forth the doctrines of the Church. He wrote, too, a Latin grammar for children, endearingly direct in its preface: "I, Aelfric, as one of but slight wisdom, have chosen these extracts and have translated them into your own language for you little boys . . . that you may be able to receive both languages into your tender minds while you progress toward higher studies."

And upon that medieval courtesy the river rests awhile, before delving even more deeply into a future that is also its past.

XII

THE STRIPLING THAMES: EYNSHAM TO LECHLADE

IMMEDIATELY above Swinford Bridge the river becomes so zany that the towing-path travels three hundred yards in order to advance by one hundred feet. It also manages to lose itself in a coppice, from which you must cross a meadow onto the highroad on the left, where a signpost—a few yards ahead on the right—points to Pinkhill Lock. Even five years ago this was a pleasant lock, islanded among fields and a wooded by-stream. Now it confronts a waterworks, and beyond that an outpost of bungolia.

It was here that I once spent a sunny afternoon, watching the Thames Conservancy men clearing the fairway. The Thames, by the way, is divided into four districts, each with an inspector and assistant inspector under a chief navigation inspector at Reading. Their work is varied. They maintain locks and they appoint water bailiffs who protect the fisheries. They regulate the water level, remove sunken vessels, grant licence for works in the river, keep the towing-path clear, levy tolls on river craft, register house-boats and pleasure boats, and prevent pollution of the river. Ten Thames Conservancy launches assist in these tasks. The Board's revenue comes chiefly from navigation fees and from various water companies.

Millions of people draw their domestic water supply from the Thames. The greatest daily discharge was recorded during the floods of 1894 which produced 20,236,000,000 gallons. No one has measured the width of the Thames at various places between Teddington and Lechlade, but everyone who has followed its course will have observed two facts: first, the width of the river at Teddington is much the same as it is at Windsor; second, the width at Eynsham (though considerably less than at Great Marlow) is much as it is at Lechlade.

After Pinkhill, meanwhile, the Thames continues (for perhaps a couple of miles) through level pastures among many trees against a background of wooded hills. And suddenly you are aware of the climax of a process which began at Bourne End, became conspicuous at Fawley, and at Goring was irresistible: now at last you are in deep country, and the Thames itself, though still a river, is almost slim enough to be called a stream. To see a rowing boat here is rare; even the cabin cruisers dwindle and proceed cautiously.

Presently you sight a phalanx of poplars on the right bank, as it were presenting arms while the Thames enters yet another of its classic reaches.

Now, some places have become famous because of a series of regional novels; others, because of one poem; but this place lives by one line of one poem:

> Crossing the stripling Thames at Bab-lock-hithe.

So wrote Matthew Arnold, of the scholar gipsy who came here in the years when Oxford meant the Gown rather than the Town. Arnold was a desiccated man whose lyric vein withered in a drought of scepticism. Even the least elegiac of his moods ends with "the eternal note of sadness". In *The Scholar Gipsy*, however, he does catch the very timbre of the medieval Thames, as when the scholar gipsy, roaming the Cumnor Hills,

> Turn'd once to watch, while thick the snowflakes fall,
> The line of festal lights in Christ Church hall. . . .

Bablock Hythe was originally spelled as *Babballacu-hyth*, meaning "the landing place at Babba's stream". Were Babba to revisit his stream he would not approve the car park, the shacks, the caravans.

Here the towing-path crosses from Oxfordshire into Berkshire. In 1279 the ferryman was named Cocus; in 1967 an ugly landing-craft serves as a car ferry. Two detours are to be recommended from Bablock Hythe; first to Stanton Harcourt on the Oxfordshire bank.

Stanton Harcourt, a village of stone houses and thatched cottages, has an admirable housing estate (showing what can be achieved in native stone) and a contemptible housing estate (showing what can be perpetrated with breeze-blocks). The Red Book of the Exchequer states that in 1166 the lands were held by Richard de Harecurt (*Ricardo fil Will*, as the scribe dubbed him). The prefix Stanton means *stan tun*, "the settlement on stony ground". There are, in fact, three monoliths in a field nearby, which may be the remains of a Druid circle.

The Norman church has an oak chancel-screen with its thirteenth-century doors, bolt, lock, key. A brass plate announces that the Harcourts were descended from a ninth-century Dane called Bernard; an hypothesis which one is disinclined either to question or to confirm. There is a splendid effigy (1394) of the Lady Maud Harcourt; and the tomb of Sir Robert Harcourt (Standard Bearer to Henry Tudor at Bosworth) and of his wife, the Lady Margaret (she, like the Duchess at Ewelme, wearing the Garter on her arm). Sir Robert wears red armour; above him hang his helmet and some shreds from a flag which may have been his personal banner. Nearby is the tomb of a twentieth-century Harcourt, Sir William, who, as Chancellor of the Exchequer, introduced the tax on death. Another tomb bears a tribute from Pope to the first Viscount Harcourt and his son:

Here lies the friend most loved, the son most dear.

But Pope did not confine his alexandrines to the nobility. When John Hewet and his fiancée were killed by lightning while reaping the harvest, Pope composed for them an epitaph so bad that charity declines to quote it.

As we discovered at Nuneham Courtenay, the manor house here was demolished during the late eighteenth century, except for its Tudor gate-house, the medieval kitchens, and a tower which housed a chapel and the chaplain's lodgings. This tower became known as Pope's Tower because the poet lived in it for several months, after the family had moved to Nuneham Courtenay. He is said to have scratched an inscription on a window pane: "In the year 1718 Alexander Pope finished here the fifth volume of Homer." That terse statement conceals a drama of bookmanship, for Pope's translation of the fifth book of *The Iliad* appeared only forty-eight hours before a rival version.

The second detour from Bablock Hythe begins on the Berkshire side, where an enchanting lane climbs to the hamlet of Eaton, a benediction of thatch and stone, with one or two modern houses of excellent texture and design. The Eight Bells also fits the picture; its name harking downstream to London River.

Beyond Bablock Hythe the Thames advances between woods on the left, and corn on the right, some of it growing within three feet of the water. Here, on a summer morning early, you will have the river to yourself, and may retain it almost intact throughout the day, for the boats above Oxford are few, and in any event a chugging launch, or some cows, or two farmfolk equating the weather with the Government are an extension of that middling privacy which is poised between solipsism and a dread of losing sight of the herd. Among these riverside wheatfields you overhear Traherne of Teddington—telling of his own corn in Herefordshire long ago: "The corn was orient and immortal wheat, which never should be reaped, nor was ever sown. I thought it had stood from everlasting to everlasting. . . . Eternity was manifest in the light of day, and some thing infinite behind every thing appeared."

For the next couple of miles the river avoids all buildings except a half-hidden cottage or farmstead. No lane leads leftward into Appleton (whose manor was once held by Thomas Chaucer of Ewelme) nor rightward into Northmoor (where the church contains the tomb of Edmund Warcupp, nephew of Mr. Speaker Lenthall, who hailed Sir Thomas Fairfax as Agamemnon, and afterwards likened him to Achilles skulking in his tent).

Appleton was the home of Edmund Dickinson—his father was rector here—whom John Evelyn described as ". . . very learned . . . lives retired, being very old and infirm, yet continuing chemistry." In the days of his strength Edmund Dickinson became physician to Charles II, and had his own laboratory in the Palace. Appleton manor-house claims to be the oldest in Berkshire; parts of it were built not later than the early thirteenth century. The church contains the tomb of a lord of the manor—one of the Fettiplace family—whom Queen Elizabeth I knighted during her progress through Oxfordshire.

At this point one feature of the river becomes conspicuous—the riverfolk, whose absence we noted in Sylvan Suburbia. By riverfolk I do not mean the traders who live off the visitors, but rather the people for whom the river is a part of their everyday lives throughout the year. To most riverside residents below

Henley-on-Thames the river is simply a pleasant view and agreeable walking or boating. Even at Oxford one is aware of the volume of summer pleasure-craft. But in this countryside the weekday Thames is primarily the companion of farmfolk and gamekeepers; and above Cricklade it will become nothing else.

A mile or so beyond Northmoor Lock a bridge has replaced a weir; and nearby stands a thatched cottage which may have been the home of the weir keeper, a man named Rudge, who had a pretty daughter.

One day—or two centuries ago, if you prefer—an undergraduate from Christ Church came fishing at this weir, and saw Betty Rudge. She—the thing has happened before and seems likely to recur—saw him. And each being well-pleased with the other, both fell in love. The undergraduate, however, happened to be William Flower, Viscount Ashbrook. But the youth did not give up, nor the maiden give in. On the contrary, her lover (as though anticipating Sabine Baring-Gould) sent his unpolished lady to be smoothed in a gentleman's family; and in 1716 the couple were married at Northmoor church.

When her husband died, twenty years later, the Viscountess married a Welsh theologian, Dr. John Johns of Jesus College, Oxford. One of her grand-daughters by the first marriage married the Duke of Marlborough, from which it follows that Sir Winston Spencer-Churchill was intrinsically a Rudge.

Northmoor, the next north bank hamlet, has a small Norman church and a Tudor house which used to be the rectory. Nearby, a modern dove-cote forms an archway above a track leading into the fields. Dove-cotes were at one time a feature of the Thames, and for that reason the word "dove" deserves to be defined. It means, among other things a pigeon. The extinct Dodo was a member of the same family, *Columbae*, which includes four British species—turtle-dove, stock-dove, wood-pigeon (or ringdove) and rock-dove (from which many of the breeds of domesticated pigeons were derived). How often, as the floods receded, must these riverside folk have sung a hymn that is both ancient and modern: "For, lo, the winter is past, the rain is over and gone; the flowers appear on the earth; the time of the singing of birds is come, and the voice of the turtle is heard in our land. . . ."

During the middle ages the right to maintain a dove-cote or *columbarium* was reserved for rectors, lords of a manor, and heads of a monastery. Nor were such birds solely an ornament, for pigeon's dung was rated the richest of all top-dressings. Even more important, the pigeon provided fresh meat with which to leaven a wintry diet of salted meat. But they were useful also as messengers, able to fly a thousand miles to their home (in 1896 a pigeon flew from Thurso to London at an average speed of fifty-five miles an hour). Queen Elizabeth I repealed the restrictive pigeon laws, and during her reign there were more than 20,000 dove-cotes in England. These declined when the Earl of Leicester helped to establish the turnips and swedes which made it possible to eat fresh meat throughout the year. But the farmers were slow to follow his example.

Passing Appleton Lower Common, the river veers from south-west to north-west through farmland towards New Bridge, which happens to be the oldest on the river, but received its name because it was made next after Radcot Bridge, whose super-structure has been rebuilt. This New Bridge dates from about the year 1250, and was enlarged two centuries later. Its arches curve to a leisurely point, as though to confirm the tempo and timbre hereabouts. They also serve as a ferry, for here the towing-path crosses into Berkshire.

Two old inns exact their toll of thirsty travellers over and under New Bridge. The Oxfordshire inn is "The Rose Revived", the Berkshire inn is "The Maybush". The former, though built of stone, looks sophisticated; but the latter retains its identity as a tavern. Indeed, it is part of the bridge itself. You step down into it, and then look up out of it, to the parapet above. It is difficult to believe that "The Maybush" is in the same county as Maidenhead and Ascot. Here nothing is to be seen except pastures, and some fields of corn or roots, and the River Windrush joining the Thames with the latest river-gossip from the Cotswolds. Here I invite you to do what I once did, which is to get lost in a maze of lanes, tracks, cows, trees, and birds which lead the good life between New Bridge and Shifford. Follow the road inland to Standlake, and afterwards the lane from Standlake to Bampton, taking care to turn left at the second of two lanes, which is sign-posted to Cote. Thereafter you may reach Shifford.

More likely you will not reach Shifford, but find yourself at Cote, which is a non-conforming sort of place having a Baptist chapel of 1664—plain, pleasant, with a gallery around three of its walls. Baptistry is strong hereabouts, and this remote hamlet was among the earliest outposts of Protestantism, for here came the Lollards, or Wyclif's "poor preachers", proclaiming a translation of the Bible which he began in 1380. Four years later it was revised by John Purvey in a more popular version, containing a prayer for all who suffer persecution: "God graunte to us alle grace to kunne (know) wel and kepe wel holi writ, and suffre ioiefulli sum peyne for it at the last" . . . as indeed many of them did. It was almost within sight of the Thames at Oxford that Bishop Latimer turned to Bishop Ridley, as they were about to be burned alive, and called out to him: "Be of good cheer, Master Ridley, and play the man. We shall this day by God's grace light such a candle in England, as I trust shall never be put out."

Shifford—or Old Shifford as the signpost names it—stands south of Cote; and one cannot easily decide which is the more conspicuous—the smallness or the isolation. Here you have passed the back-of-beyond, and are in a riverside terrain so remote that it has no shop, no pub, nothing larger than four houses at a time, all served by the sort of roads which even a countryman would describe as narrow lanes.

At Shifford, it is said, the first English Parliament was summoned; which seems probable if you define "Parliament" to fit the occasion. East Shefford, in Berkshire, also claims this distinction, but the chronicler wrote "Shifford". He also wrote: "At Shifford there sat many thanes . . . and Alfred, England's herdsman, England's darling. He was King in England, and he taught them that could hear him, how they should live." Once a royal borough with sixteen churches, Shifford is now a fistful of cottages: so passed Ravenna itself, once the seat of Emperors, and now, in the words of a guidebook, "a small town with glorious mosaics, near Venice".

If, by the way, you approach the river from Cote, you must follow a lane into Chimney, which contains two houses and a farm, each within a long stone's throw of the water. But only the farmer himself can direct you thither. Unless you follow his instructions, you will almost certainly fail to find the plank which carries you across swampy ground. Having walked that plank, you must turn downstream, past a weir, along half a mile of straight and high-banked river, thickly wooded on either side.

Cricklade Bridge

You pass under a bridge (not a handsome one) that must have been built for cattle because it leads only to a ford across a back-water. A couple of hundred yards below the bridge lies Shifford Lock, the loneliest on the Thames, and my own favourite. The place is so isolated that its keeper must walk to the farm at Chimney in order to collect his household supplies. Coal and heavier equipment arrive by water.

At Shifford there is the river, there is the lock cottage, there is a hinterland of meadows and the myriad inhabitants thereof; but anything else is, as the Bible succinctly puts it, not. Here you may begin to live by starting to hear the sounds of living—a breeze, for example, and the river itself, and (if your ears are keen) the murmur of growing grass—even, perhaps, the sound which this planet makes while it spins on its axis through an orbit.

Just below Shifford the towing-path crosses from Berkshire into Oxfordshire; just above Shifford the sylvania gives way to an unusually treeless reach. Here the river sprawls through meadows that may remain damp throughout the summer.

Presently, however, the Berkshire Downs loom up on the left, topped by a tower which Lord Berners built in 1936, presumably because he liked the look of it. Having passed under an attractive timber bridge, called Tenfoot, the river re-acquires its trees; and so continues through the unoccupied England, under the lee of Faringdon Clump, towards Tadpole Bridge, whose single arch emphasizes how slender the stream has become. The Trout Inn waits beside the bridge; a homely place, built in 1802. No other house is visible. Southward a lane climbs leisurely to the Berkshire Downs. Northward it saunters levelly into Bampton.

Of all the towns which stand back a little from the Thames, Bampton is my favourite. Bampton-in-the-Bush they used to call it—Bush meaning a remote and timbered country. To a townsman Bampton will seem scarcely larger than a village. Its nucleus is the town hall, from which several streets and lanes splay out like spokes. The church offers a selection of styles from early Norman to late Hanoverian; much of the fabric is of the eleventh century; the reredos is fourteenth century, the brass to "a venerable and scientific man" is sixteenth century, some of the monuments are seventeenth-century, the thirteenth-century octagonal tower is 170 feet high.

Aylmer de Valence built a castle here, which stood until the

11

Infant Thames at Ashton Keynes

eighteenth century. The Tudor house, known as the Deanery, still does stand, recording that it once belonged to the Deans of Exeter, who still hold the advowson. That west country link was forged by a Bampton man, Leofric, first Bishop of Exeter. But to litanize every house would seem a supererogation of unnecessity; Bampton is a home, not a museum. Its shops shine and are up-to-date, though never so unsociably modern that they invite you to serve yourself. Women who live in deep country, spending much of the day alone or with small children, expect to gossip when they go shopping. Above all, they demand to be waited on for a change.

Bampton has two annual galas. One of them is the horse fair which was granted by Edward I to William of Valence, but has been overshadowed by its famous namesake in Devon; the other is the Whit Monday Morris dancing, done with such gusto, against so gracious a background, that it comes alive and stops the mouth of anachronism. The Morris dancers are escorted by an attendant whose sword carries a cake; in less sublimated years it carried a hunk of venison, and all who cared to ask received a cut from the joint.

Bampton owes its well-being to the absence of a main road. Such roads as do pass through lead from anywhere-in-general to nowhere-in-particular. In other words, Bampton maintains a high standard of living. Even on a summer Saturday you can hear yourself think in Bampton. You can cross the street without needing to look for a motorist who is travelling so fast that he cannot halt in time to give way. One September afternoon I sat on the steps of the town hall, eating sandwiches while counting cars: no vehicle passed through in eighteen minutes, and only three appeared in half-an-hour. That alone is sufficient reason for saying of Bampton what Belloc wrote of Sussex: "May it stand forever despite petrol. . . ."

During all this time the river has been flowing steadily westward, proceeded and preceded by the Great Brook (which runs between Shifford and Rushy Lock) and by the Sharney and Burroway Brooks (which run from Rushy to Radcot Locks). At Rushy Lock the keeper's cottage disproves the rule that all Victorian architecture is either ugly or inept. This cottage was built in 1896, with simple good sense.

Inland on the left stands Faringdon, the only Berkshire stone town, and only because it waits on the Cotswolds' doorstep. As at Wallingford, an ancient market house perches on pillars, near a cruciform church of the thirteenth century. Faringdon produced Henry Pye, one of the five Poets Laureate who lived near the Thames.

Henry James Pye went up to Magdalen College, Oxford, in 1762; in which year also he composed an *Ode on the Birth Day of the Prince of Wales* (not to be recommended, nor the Prince neither). Shortly after Pye had come of age, his father died, bequeathing to him the family seat, Faringdon Hall, together with debts of £50,000. Undaunted, the boy that same year married and lived happily for three decades thereafter.

Pye was prolix as well as prolific. His contributions to the literature of the Thames include one of the then-fashionable topographical poems, *Faringdon Hill*, from whose eminence he discovered that

> Here SOL intensely glows, and there the trees
> Exclude the cool refreshment of the breeze,

as a result of which,

> Come let us quit these scenes, and climb yon brow,
> Yon airy summit where the ZEPHYRS blow.

That was in 1772. Sixteen years later Wordsworth launched the great preface to his *Lyrical Ballads*, with a right hook flashing out from round one, paragraph one: "They who have been accustomed to the gaudiest and inane phraseology of many modern writers. . . ." However, it can be said of Pye that he eschewed absinthe, steered clear of Grub Street, and enjoyed the life of a country gentleman so well that he wrote a poem—*Shooting*—which states that in August the guns are got ready. Pye made rather more of it than that:

> When the last sun of August's fiery reign
> Now bathes his radiant forehead in the main,
> The panoply by sportive heroes worn
> Is rang'd in order for the ensuing morn.

In 1807 Pye indulged his sportsmanship more fully, by publishing "an improved and enlarged" edition of *The Sportsman's Dictionary*, whose title at least must have taken away the reader's breath:

The Sportsman's Dictionary containing Instructions for Various Methods to be Observed in Riding, Hunting, Fowling, Setting, Fishing, Racing, Farriery, Hawking, Breeding and Feeding Horses for the Road and Turf; the management of Dogs, Game and Dunghill-Cocks, Turkeys, Geese, Ducks, Doves, Singing-Birds etc; and the manner of curing their various diseases and accidents.

Pye served as Justice of the Peace at Faringdon, but not always gladly, for Leigh Hunt said that he once saw Pye "in a state of scornful indignation at being interrupted in the perusal of a manuscript by the monitions of his police-officers, who were obliged to remind him over and over again that he was a magistrate, and that the criminal multitude were in waiting. . . ."

Pye, finally, wrote a bad play on a good theme, King Alfred, in which that monarch, disguised as a peasant, is discovered by one of his subjects (a woman named Egga) brooding before a fire that has burned her cakes. The text of the play continues as follows:

(Enter Egga from behind)
Egga. Whew! They're cinders!

Egga then "offers to strike him". Happily, Thane Ethelnoth enters, crying, "O king, O blessed hour!" Pye seems not to have accepted the legend that the cakes were a total loss, for presently Egga's daughter enters and, having retrieved the cakes, assures her mother: ". . . they're but a trifle singed!"

And so to Radcot, which is less a place than a place-name, though the name itself shows that Radcot's cottages were formerly thatched with *rad* or reed. Nowadays the only riverside buildings are the inn and two bridges, marked by magnificent poplars. The smaller bridge was built in 1787 for the Cut that was to take extra traffic from the Thames and Severn Canal. The larger, spanning a by-stream, is said to have witnessed a baronial skirmish in 1387. The central arch has a socket that once held a cross (bridges and roads being at that time in the care of the Church). This unpeopled place used to be an important wharf, from which the Cotswold stone was shipped down-river for the making of Wren's cathedral.

Having turned north, west and north again, the river holds to its purpose of not entering even the smallest of hamlets. You can walk or scull for hours, not sighting a chimney, not hearing a car, and holding only such conversation as is to be had of cattle, sheep, birds, and the leisurely men whose business lies among them.

"History," said the late Henry Ford, "is bunk"—a proposition which resembles the men who propound it. Nevertheless, there are moments when one would rather hear a blackbird, or count the catkins, than visit even the noblest church or the most impressive birthplace. At Kelmscot, however, you have simply to tether your boat and step ashore, for the village, though invisible, trickles almost to the water's edge.

In days gone by Cenhelm came here, and built a cot, and baptized a community as *Cenhelm's Cot*. Centuries later William Morris came here, and bought the Manor, and made it famous. But Morris was no week-ender who discovered Kelmscot by chance. He had loved it before he came to possess it.

William Morris was born at Walthamstow, in 1834, when that place was a village. He came of the cultivated bourgeoisie whom Marx despised as the acid of the earth. At Exeter College, Oxford he read widely, helped to found *The Oxford and Cambridge Magazine*, and in 1856 resigned in order to practise the preaching of Rossetti and Ruskin. He became, in fact, a craftsman who designed and sometimes made his own furniture. He founded the Society for the Preservation of Ancient Buildings. He launched the Kelmscott Press, whose binding and typography led the world. He financed a firm that made handsome furniture. He wrote stories about Viking pirates and medieval knights.

His old home, the Manor House, never was a manor house, because no *seigneur* ever lived there. It stands within a few yards of the river, only its roof visible above trees and a high wall. Morris's daughter, May, bequeathed it as a retreat for Oxford dons, but so few of them ever advanced thither that the house was leased to a friend of the family, on condition that visitors were allowed to inspect it. In 1966 it was extensively renovated. Among the contents are some of the tapestries woven by Morris, several wallpapers designed by him, and a sketch of Mrs. Morris by her too-fervent admirer, Rossetti.

The house itself is a blend of mid-Tudor and early Jacobean, and was at one time owned by a yeoman family named Turner. The uppermost rooms are framed against resolute oak and elm. When Morris repaired the house, he used local stone, local timber, and nails that were made by the village blacksmith. In the yard is another Thames dove-cote, a seventeenth-century work of artistry, with whitewashed walls and black nesting-places. Having seen Kelmscot Manor one understands why Morris declared: "As others love the race of man through their lover or their children, so I love the earth through this small space of it."

Perhaps, after all, the best approach to Kelmscot is by land, because that way will reveal its seclusion, down a long lane off a minor road. And you must proceed on foot, that being the proper pace at which to savour the details and to imbibe the peace.

The hub of this small universe is a pub, "The Plough", which is also the shop. In front of it stands the base of a market cross; and all around are stone houses; some, exceedingly beautiful; others, content to seem homely. This is a farming community. Wisps of straw adorn the lane, jettisoned from wagons. Dung is dropped, to smell sweeter than petrol. Only once have I seen a car here, and that contained a pig, a child, two cairns, and (I never asked why) a man fast asleep.

Kelmscot church stands inland, at the end of an avenue of limes. Its bell-cote was made in 1300, to compensate for lack of a tower. A thirteenth-century window-frame contains some fifteenth-century glass showing Saint George and his *bête noir*, above a velvet cloth brocaded with roses, which Mrs. William Morris gave to the parish. Morris himself died at Hammersmith, and is commemorated by the William Morris Gallery in Walthamstow, but he was buried at Kelmscot. A stanza by Morris describes the impact of this quiet and memorable place:

> Then rose his heart, and cleared his brow,
> And slow he rode his way:
> As then it was, so is it now,
> Not all hath worn away.

Not worn away is true, because at Kelmscot you become aware that your relationship with the river has matured, which is to say has augmented itself. From the very start the Thames evoked admiration; at Hampton Court, by Windsor Castle, through Cliveden Reach the admiration may have widened into affection; and above Great Marlow it became friendship. The friendship, I suggest, grew stronger, and at Kelmscot you recognize that it has become deep affection, even perhaps love, based upon old acquaintance and the remembrance of many tangible attractions . . . the backwater at Cookham, the woods above Fawley, a morning in Mapledurham, hours beside Masefield's river at Clifton Hampden, the murmur of rushes that will never again lighten Eynsham's darkness. And this empathy, this tenderness, is heightened because the Thames has grown quieter, narrower, more intimate. Idealization, however, is out—right out—of the question. The Thames at Kelmscot can behave outrageously, even towards Morris's home, which it has more than once flooded. Until the river was effectively banked during the nineteenth century, this part of it suffered severe floods. Cows swam over walls beside the lane, and on one occasion the villagers were marooned upstairs for six weeks; food having to be ferried, and hoisted on the end of a pitchfork. The worst summer flood of the twentieth century occurred in June, 1903, when the hay was destroyed, and young Kelmscoters took to diving into the lane from the cross beside "The Plough". During the floods of January, 1915, some 1,760,000,000 gallons of water raced through Eaton Weir, a mile downstream.

Of the original village of Eaton Hastings nothing remains except the small church, a cottage or two, and Town Meadow, marking the site of the medieval village. Old people hereabouts still refer to Eaton Weir as Hart's Weir, Hart being the name of an innkeeper who turned smuggler. He bought his spirits from bargemen, and then hid it in kegs chained to the river-bed. Hart really was a moonraker because he supplied his customers after dark, using a rake to retrieve the kegs.

Buscot, the next Berkshire place, looks older than it is, having been designed as a model village in 1879. Most of its trim cottages are of stone or brick, sprinkled with thatched houses from the earlier village.

Buscot Park and its house lie a mile inland, nearly four hundred feet up, with a reservoir and a lake. It was given to the National Trust by Lord Faringdon. The riverside rectory is a handsome eighteenth-century mansion of the middling sort.

At Buscot House lived Squire Campbell, who made his village famous throughout the country of the Thames. He it was who dug the reservoir, designed the lake, brought hundreds of acres under cultivation, built a distillery beside the river, and used steam ploughs which worked throughout the day and night, lit by limelights. The reservoir cost, in modern currency, £100,000;

and an Act of Parliament had to be passed in order to allow
Squire Campbell to erect a pumping station by the river. This
station irrigated his lands, and supplied the tenants with water.
Its wheel was sixteen feet wide, and weighed twenty-five tons. At
a time when farm-hands were fortunate if they worked less than
twelve hours a day, Squire Campbell's men worked for nine
hours. Campbell himself was out and about in all weathers, often
accompanied through the fields by his lady, who hitched her
skirts to a belt.

From Buscot village a track leads to the river (reserved, says a
sign, for farmers and water-worksmen). I trespass here in order to
admire the solitary farmhouse and a cottage beside the foaming
weir. The banks are as tall as a man, offering shade in summer and
a windbreak in winter. This is the highest point at which I ever
saw a sailing boat. Above Buscot the navigable depth of water in
summer is three feet. The Buscot lock-keeper is usually to be
found at the next lock. That is the extent to which the Thames has
ceased to be a pleasure ground.

Now the river backs due east, and then turns on itself as though
intent to leave no stone unturned on a twice-trodden avenue.
After that, it heads west into a memorable vista. First, however, it
passes Saint John's Bridge, where the River Leach joins in,
baptizing Lechlade.

Saint John's Bridge is a nineteenth-century superstructure on
thirteenth-century foundations. At its northern end stands the
Trout Inn, on the site of a priory of Black Monks who tended the
sick. The priory walls were intact during the eighteenth century,
and within them the local overseers built a workhouse, which was
demolished in 1795. The landlord at "The Trout" will direct you
to the remains of the priory.

The Trout Inn was formerly called the Saint John Baptist's
Head, a grisly title, changed in 1704 to the present appropriately
piscatorial sign. The medieval priors received local fishing rights
from King John, and these now belong to "The Trout". Just
beyond the inn, a lane leads rightward into Kelmscot.

Now turn from the pub, and lean on the parapet, looking towards Lechlade. Immediately below you, the highest lock on the
river maintains the Conservancy's motto of seamanlike trimness.
To the right, the road sweeps through a wide arc into the town.
Ahead, the roofs of that town shimmer in sunlight, or wear

winter's halo of pastel smoke: and above them shines the spire of the parish church, graceful as the topmost tier on a wedding cake.

At Lechlade the Thames enters a new phase of its life. Here four counties meet—Berkshire, Oxfordshire, Wiltshire, Gloucestershire—so that the river leaves the southern shires, and enters the West of England. If it were not a reversal of truth, you would say that at Lechlade the river shows the first symptoms of extreme old age—an outward paring-away, an inner serenity which can be gently gay.

Leaving, then, the highest lock, with Lechlade spire ahead, steady as the Pole Star, the river enters Lechlade, past the little wharf which now shelters a few cabin cruisers, but was once a port-of-call for barges from many parts of the south and west. A hundred craft would lie-up between Saint John's Lock and the town bridge, the largest of them laden with eighty tons of mixed merchandise. During the early years of the nineteenth century Lechlade handled a cargo so various that it included cannon and cheese, nails and iron, artillery shells and raw hide. Of the local cheese industry Defoe remarked: "A vast quantity is every week . . . carried to the river of Thames, which runs through part of the country, by land carriage and so by barges to London." The famous Single Gloucester cheese was made once a day, from the previous evening's milk; and since it ripened within six weeks, it offered a relatively quick return to the dairy farmer. By the end of the seventeenth century Lechlade wharves were handling three thousand tons of local cheese a year.

Lechlade Bridge is hump-backed and narrow, branded nowadays by traffic lights. The townsfolk built it in 1792, to replace a ferry. The toll was a halfpenny for pedestrians, whence the name Halfpenny Bridge. The snug toll-house survives, like its fellow at Eynsham. Unfortunately, the bridge bears a heavy load of traffic to and from neighbouring quarries and gravel pits, which, with the holiday motorists, mar the riverside amenities.

The manor of Lechlade was held by many of history's household names, among them Richard Plantagenet, Earl of Cornwall, who, having declined the Crown of Sicily, became Holy Roman Emperor—the only Englishman ever to wear that imperial purple. Other lords of Lechlade were Edwin Mortimer, Earl of March; and Richard, Duke of York, who fathered two English kings.

Lechlade has many fine stone houses and a few thatched ones, with yet another of the early Baptist chapels (1817) which confirm an indigenous nonconformity. And behind the Crown Inn is another splendid dove-cote.

The parish church of Saint Lawrence was built by the vicar of an earlier church, one Conrad Ney, in or about 1474. Its porch was made of stones taken from the priory of Saint John. A modern font—the work of local masons—stands on a fourteenth-century base which, they say, was found in a nearby garden. But it is the spire that catches the eye, as Shelley observed on a September afternoon, at an hour when

> The wind has swept from the wide atmosphere
> Each vapour that obscured the sunset's ray. . . .

Lechlade is in Gloucestershire, but if you feel inclined to wander a few miles into Oxfordshire, you will find, at the village of Windrush, a unique church. Its walls contain two Norman archways and three thirteenth-century windows, but the building itself has long been an inhabited cottage. The village postman knows it as Number 88.

Lechlade used to hold two annual fairs: one on St. John the Baptist's Day, the other (a horse fair) in September. They still do hold a mixed fair, of the sort which Masefield has described: "The square was crowded with the booths of merchants, most of them selling crockery, decorative china, usually pink and gold, or cakes, fruit, and hard-bake, all three glistening with stickiness. Four shows were busy; a merry-go-round, with a steam organ; a merry-go-round with a steam organ and cymbals; a smaller merry-go-round with a trumpeter and drummer; and a double stand of swing boats." There are old people who still remember Masefield's next scene: "In the northern side of the square, close to the church, there was a hiring stand, where a few men and women hung about still hoping to be hired." That was not an equitable way of dividing labour, and now it has gone for good, together with several other bad things. But the Cotswolds craftsmen have not gone. The Town Centre is a memorial to what they have achieved, and an augur of what they will achieve. Lechlade stonemason's yard will delight everyone whose eye and hand respond to craftsmanship. I once spent a rich half-hour here, listening while a Gloucestershire mason compared notes with a Peakland mason, his brother-in-law, in the presence of their elder sons, who also were masons. Small sections of limestone were exchanged, a chisel was produced, and presently the sparks flew upward as the two craftsmen practised their own preaching; the sons standing by, better able than I to assess the skill, but not less marvelling at their fathers' mastery of it. Then indeed I saw a version of the expertise which Robert Bridges observed among athletes:

> They that in play can do the things they would,
> Having an instinct throned in reason's place. . . .

Beyond Lechlade only the smallest craft will venture, for the draught dwindles to a couple of feet. Lechlade, in fact, is both the beginning and the end of the river's cruising ground. Immediately above the bridge (which has aged prematurely and looks the better for it) a small wharf attracts no more customers than seem companionable. On the opposite shore, along the towing-path, not too many people bask, bathe, fish, saunter, sleep; contriving to do these things so amiably that only a churlish eremite could wish them away from the scene, and himself (in Traherne's phrase) "the only spectator and enjoyer of it". But, as I have said, all this is deafened by the spate of summer traffic.

At Lechlade the beginning and the end of the boating season can be savoured more vividly because more intimately than anywhere else in the Thames. Although he wrote as a seaman for seamen, Quiller-Couch composed the finest of all elegies upon the boatman's *fin de siècle*: "There arrives a day towards the end of October—or with luck we may tide it over into November—when the wind in the mainsail suddenly takes a winter force, and we begin to talk of laying up the boat. . . . This ritual of laying up the boat is our way of bidding farewell to summer; and we go through it, when the day comes, in ceremonial silence." Many a Thames mariner will respond to Quiller-Couch's salt-water nostalgia as he casts a farewell glance at his winter-berthed boat: "As we thread our way homeward among the riding-lights flickering on black water, the last pale vision of her alone and lightless follows and reminds me of the dull winter ahead, the short days, the long nights. She is haunting me yet as I land on the wet slip strewn with dead leaves to the tide's edge. She follows me up the hill, and even to my library door." But Quiller-Couch eschewed Arnold's "eternal note of sadness", for when he opened his library door: "Lo, a bright fire burning, and, smiling over against the blaze of it, cheerful, companionable, my books have been waiting for me."

And cheerful, too, the spring mornings at Lechlade, when the countryfolk come down to launch their hibernating boat. This is the happiest of all the portrait's smiling features, with farm-worn and desk-bound fathers transformed to seem the very heirs of Drake and Nelson—and of John Cabot, too—born to rule and once again explore the wavelets.

Nor is the cruising man the "only spectator and enjoyer" of Lechlade in spring. Those others, who live up-river, along the boatless reaches that await us—they too lift up their hearts, for now, in the beautifully spare lines of C. Day Lewis,

> Now the full-throated daffodils
> Our trumpeters in gold,
> Call resurrection from the ground
> And bid the year be bold.

From ourselves also a grain of boldness is required, for as we leave Lechlade, and scan the narrowing stream, we overhear our own question: "How many more miles before we must step ashore because there is no longer enough water to keep us afloat?"

XIII

THE SOUND OF WINTER: AN INTERLUDE

TONIGHT brings the first hard frost, which coincides with a full moon, and is therefore startling. The river seems so white that for a moment you suppose you had never before seen moonlight; but when you tread the towing-path—crinkling like tissue paper —you understand that the moon holds only half the credit; the rest belongs to the frost.

Unlike the stars, which are already waning, all branches are motionless, pinned to the ground by moonlight. Everywhere being white, it is as though all farmers had sown the same celestial crop. After a while, however, ploughland beside the river identifies itself by means of the flints, which speak like ships at night. Woods are easily recognizable. They stand astride the hills, and are darker than black. Through them the stars appear, rising and falling while you walk, and halting whenever you stop. When a breeze shivers a branch, the stars trickle like raindrops from a twig.

At the farm across the river a light is switched on, swifter than surprise. You invent reasons for it. Lovers? Illness reaching a crisis? Babies crying? Old age cursing its bladder? Now the light goes out, quick as it came on. Perhaps, after all, it had not signified. Yet, for a few moments more, you wonder. Lamplight in the countryside is rare after midnight.

The lock's timber gate appears to have been sprinkled with sugar, each granule a gem. But when you touch it, the sugar-icing turns sour, prickling a bare thumb; and when you touch it again, you discover that moonlight is indelible. Ghostliest of all is the lock-keeper's cottage. Its windows flaunt silver flames, and the tiles glint like square shillings.

Unlike the tiles, puddles do not glint; they glower, duller than gun-metal, and when you puncture one it turns opaque, like a shattered wind-screen. A leaf tinkles to the frozen water, bouncing instead of bending at the impact. Then it snaps in half, brittle as burned toast.

Sometimes a pistol-shot rings out, fired by a horse lumbering across the fields, each frozen puddle uttering its salvo. Yesterday that field was a Sargasso; tonight its channels are cliffs. Nozzling some hay, the horse bites off more than it can chew, for the stuff is matted, and comes up by the yard, crackling.

When you stand still, the meadows speak. In them you hear hares—or a stoat, or a cat, or a weasel—nocturnalling among iced nettles. Another leaf falls, striking the river with a clink quieter than *pianissimo*.

Now a swan collapses on the ice, like a tipsy ballerina past her prime, showing the withered shins. Up-river someone utters a groan, and then you remember that it must be the dinghy, caught in the ice.

At the far end of the bridge a roadman's hurricane-lamp marks an obstruction. The flame burns steadily, and in the stillness the paraffin talks to itself, loud enough for you to hear. A heap of coal for the brazier shines white, like nothing on earth.

All the while, this frost—which slays birds, torments animals, splices trees, and would, if it could, petrify humanity itself—all the while, this same malignant frost is crumbling the soil in a benevolent vice, breaking down the clods, so that air and moisture may circulate freely.

Suddenly that second leaf, which has strayed to the edge of the ice, is caught by a brief breeze, and launched upon Lethe. You watch it as it glides into the unreturning darkness and is lost. Or is it? Twenty yards down-stream, when you arrive there, a leaf has been speared on the point of an ice-flow, swaying like an uncertain compass-needle.

Twelve weeks ago you lay beside this river, while the sun tanned your face. Even eight weeks ago you sat here, warmed by the autumn tints. Now there is only bitter cold, and the silence of things freezing, keener and keener as the night wears on:

> A cold night,
> A clear moon,
> The stars bright
> And thick strewn.

Firelight flows
From the farm
Like a rose
Keeping warm.

The sheep graze,
The mill bides,
The church prays,
The stream glides.

From the spheres
Swinging round
Silence hears
Not a sound.

This is bare
Beauty, caught
On an air
Keenly wrought.

XIV

COTSWOLD COUNTRY: LECHLADE TO KEMBLE

"ENOUGH water to keep us afloat" . . . at Lechlade Bridge there is enough for any craft drawing less than two-and-a-half feet; but one of those feet will soon be amputated, and after three or four miles even the other limb must begin to lose its toes.

Until that happens, the river above Lechlade bears southward, with a loud main road to port, and the old Thames and Severn Canal to starboard, plus the River Coln, which joins the main-stream.

In a little while the road falls out of sight, then out of hearing, and finally out of mind, leaving you among meadows as bucolic as Mopsa. On the south bank Inglesham church is just visible through the trees. If you do land here, you will step ashore in Wiltshire. The church—it is nine centuries old, and was presented to the Abbot of Beaulieu by King John—stands some distance from the highway, to which it is joined by a track passing through a farm. Unlike many restored churches, this one retains its true identity, and an inscription on the wall explains why: "This Church was repaired in 1888–9 through the energy and with the help of William Morris who loved it." According to my reckon-ing, the chancel is less than twenty-one feet long; the walls bear traces of medieval paintings. A Jacobean pulpit stands near a carving of Mary and the infant Jesus, with a heavenly hand blessing them. You may wonder why this carving is so weather-beaten. In fact, it may for centuries have stood outside the Priory of St. John the Baptist at Lechlade.

Beyond Inglesham you find yourself asking, "Is this still a river? Or has it already become a stream?" . . . questions that can best be answered by any navigator who has ignored the wise men of Lechlade, and is now aground and likely to remain there.

Leaving him to his folly, the Thames continues south and some-

Old roundhouse near Somerford Keynes

times east (which leads to Teddington) all the while accompanied by a background of hills which at Upper Inglesham reach three hundred feet.

When Quiller-Couch was exploring the Warwickshire Avon, he leaned on Eckington's ancient bridge, scanning the wheatfields; and as he leaned, a poem came to him, *Upon Eckington Bridge*, which begins

> O pastoral heart of England! like a psalm
> Of green days telling with a quiet beat. . . .

. . . to which the people of this Wiltshire Thames will say "Amen" because the description fits their own country also, not greatly changed since Camden three centuries ago portrayed it as ". . . exceedingly fertile, and plentifull of all things, yea, and for the varieties thereof, passing pleasant and delightsome." This may be called the most prehistoric of all the Thames counties; littered with stones, sites and mounds, as Collins noticed, rather too exclamatorily:

> In yonder grave a Druid lies
> Where slowly winds the stealing Wave!

Here, therefore, is a place at which to dispel some of the myths about Britons and Celts. "Britons" is a collective noun which identifies our earliest forefathers at a time before their homeland had co-opted out of Europe by becoming an island. Today the noun is more than ever useful because it placates the various patriotisms. The phrase "British Empire" was first used by Henry VIII ("empire" meaning *imperium* or governorship of these islands).

The Celts, on the other hand, were a continental people, now commonly divided into three groups—Gaulish, Cymric, Goildelic—of whom the second and third groups crossed the Channel to found respectively the Welsh, the Irish, and the Scots as an Irish offshoot. Waves of Norse, Germanic, and Norman invaders pushed the Celts further and further towards the rest of their fellows in the south-west of England. Less than three centuries ago the Cornish spoke their own Celtic language, into which all official decrees and documents were translated, and the Bible also. The Celts were a race of gaily melancholic poets whose classic monument is Stonehenge. They still are a race of poets, and in

12

Source of the Thames

southern Ireland or among the Scottish Isles they see and speak more things than are dreamed of in the heavenless earth of industrial England.

Beside its heritage of Celtic remains, this Wiltshire Thames preserves a tradition of dairy-farming. Wick, for example, is a common place-name hereabouts, from the Latin *vicus* or village, which became the Old English *wic*, and was used as a general name for a dairy-farm. Wick, in fact, is the plural of *wic*, and means therefore a place with several dairies.

The Hall near Hannington Wick is an impressive Elizabethan mansion with a pierced parapet. It stands at one end of an avenue of elms; at the other end is the church with a late medieval tower and Tudor walls. Hannington itself is scarcely a hamlet, but at one time it was large enough to support two inns—"The Dog", and "The Cat and Mouse"—which disappeared and were replaced by a farmhouse that supplied what Mr. Weller Senior might have called "Wittals with a we, my lord". A pair of stocks stood outside "The Cat and Mouse". Their last occupant is said to have been Davy Garrett, who had a wooden leg. On being stocked for drunkenness, Garrett asked permission to insert his wooden leg while keeping the native limb at liberty. This the constable refused.

The former blacksmith at Hannington was alive during the 1914 War. They called him Whistling Joe. While serving his apprenticeship down-river at Buscot, Joe had to visit Kelmscot, for a daily shoeing there. When the Thames was in flood he would strip, wrap the tools of his trade in his clothes, set the bundle on his head, and stride the sunken meadows, sometimes chest-high in water.

From Hannington a track becomes a path leading into Highworth which is still good-looking despite some modernity. This small, traffic-scarred town stands astride a hill overlooking the Thames Valley and three southern versions of Housman's "coloured counties". Highworth has two suburbs—Eastropp and Westropp—and since *trop* is a variant of the Danish *thorp*, it follows that the Danes came here, almost certainly by water. Highworth's Norman-and-Perpendicular church has been "restored". For three hours Major Hen held it as a fortress for Charles I against Fairfax's guns. A stray cannon ball was preserved in the south chapel, where a glass case contains the helmet and part of a tunic believed to have been worn by a knight crusader.

A more recent crusade is recorded by a tablet to a member of the Warneford family, which for nearly three hundred years lived at Warneford Place, in the hamlet of Sevenhampton, two miles away. In 1915 Lieutenant Warneford was flying above Belgium when he sighted a German Zeppelin. His only weapons were bombs. Seeing him, the Zeppelin let go her ballast, and soared to six thousand feet. The Lieutenant—he happened to have been educated at Shakespeare's school—climbed after the Zeppelin, and hung on there, defying her guns, until she began the descent to her base. Then he swooped, and with great skill bombed the airship. The force of the explosion turned his own aircraft upside-down, emptying the tanks. He glided to earth, refilled from reserve cans, and took-off unharmed. For destroying a Zeppelin single-handed in mid-air, Lieutenant Warneford received the Victoria Cross. A few days later he was killed in action.

Because of such men Highworth is free to enjoy its cakes and ale, though during the Harvest Festival, when most other countryfolk consume the fruits of the earth, Highworth used to observe a Lenten-like fast—not, indeed, of fish, but of rice pudding. They had, too, their own harvest song, worthy to be called a Wiltshire Psalm:

> Praise Him for the wheat sheaves, gathered safely into barn,
> And scattering now their golden drops beneath the sounding flail.
> O happy heart of this broad land, praise the God of Harvest.

A country quiet as this, with its maze of ambling lanes, invites the walker, the motorist who cares to picnic off a beaten track, and indeed every sort of open air pilgrim. Through its stillness one overhears John Bunyan's rousing voice:

> There's no discouragement
> Shall make him once relent
> His first avowed intent
> To be a pilgrim.

At Hannington Wick the river ceases to be suitable for motor traffic. Even rowing boats seem too big. Only a canoe will comfortably ride such sharply narrow bends among such reeds, shallows, and overhanging trees.

Soon after Hannington the Thames enters Gloucestershire, and turns north to Kempsford where, if you are boating, you must

moor alongside a farmhouse under the lee of the church. If, on
the other hand, you arrive by road, you must go as far as the road
goes, which is into the aforesaid farm. No right of way exists,
but the farmer offers user to men of goodwill. So, having entered
his yard, you turn sharp right, past the farmhouse—a handsome
old place, lovingly maintained. Below it flows the river—or perhaps you have already said "stream" because a dozen strokes
would carry a swimmer across and back again. Anyway, follow
the river rightward for a couple of hundred yards, passing a wall
whose gate reveals the farm garden. The grass here is greener than
the svelte lawns of sylvan suburbia, not because you wish it
so but because of the soil and its climate. A hen picks her way
among herbaceous borders. Cows cough from the far side of the
river. Robins walk the plank that was once an elm and is now a
bridge. I have stood here on a June evening when drought had
so parched the river that a child might have forded it; and I have
crouched here on a February morning when fallen branches
created audible waterfalls.

In the year 800 Kempsford spelled itself *Cynemaeres* (which
became *Kynesmersford* about the year 1200), meaning "Cynmaer's
ford". Who Cynmaer was we do not know and probably never
shall. What his descendants were like can be guessed from what
they built. Their village contains one long street flanked by a few
beautiful old houses and many ugly new ones.

Here lived John of Gaunt (or Ghent, his birthplace), fourth son
of Edward III, and the greatest of all English noblemen who
appear in this portrait. To Shakespeare he was "time-honoured
Lancaster". His first wife was Blanche, heiress to the Duchy of
Lancaster, which he inherited. When Blanche died, the Duke
built Kempsford church tower as her memorial. But she has a
monument more lasting than stone, for Chaucer was her protegé,
and he showed his gratitude by composing an elegy, *The Deth
of Blaunche the Duchesse*.

Three years later the Duke married Constance, heir to the
kingdom of Castile, so this time he became a King. His head,
however, lay uneasily under a crown, and in 1387 he renounced
Castile in favour of his daughter. Back in England, he did good
work, mending the breach between the King and nobility; and
when his second wife died he took a third, though from her he
inherited nothing—the new wife being an old mistress, Catherine

Swynford, by whom he already had several children (these were legitimised in 1397, and one of them, Bolingbroke, Earl of Derby, became Henry IV).

John of Gaunt's house decayed and was replaced by a Jacobean house which also decayed, except for a few fragments still standing beside the river.

Kempsford's is the most impressive of all churches within a few yards of the Thames. Each porch has a doorway with Norman carvings; a priest's effigy lies in the chancel, wearing robes of the late middle ages; a Flemish brass shows Walter Hickman in Tudor gown. And above them—turreted, windowed, niched— Gaunt's tower climbs in three tiers above Gloucestershire.

One of Kempsford's vicars was Dr. Woodforde, afterwards Bishop of Ely, of whom they tell a tale. Hearing a parishioner speak of his ewe-lambs, Dr. Woodforde (who must have been as urban as Dr. Johnson) remarked: "I have always read that passage as *ee-wee* lamb."

And they tell two other stories here, each about John of Gaunt's house and the river. One of the children of the first Duke of Lancaster, John of Gaunt's father-in-law, was drowned at the ford, and the father was so grieved that he left the village and never returned to it.

The second story concerns John of Gaunt's sister-in-law, the Lady Maud. Much baronial fighting took place hereabouts, and one night the Lady Maud's brother-in-law arrived at the house, seeking shelter from enemies who were already pursuing her husband in another part of the country. In order to maintain secrecy, the Lady Maud hid her guest, and at night time took food to him in his room, afterwards walking with him on the terrace. But someone in the house (from jealousy, it was said) grew suspicious of these midnight flittings, and sent word to the Earl that his wife harboured a lover, his own brother. The Earl, eluding his enemies, rode home to Kempsford, hid himself on the terrace until it was dark, and in due time surprised his wife as she walked with her guest. Without pausing to confirm a slander, the Earl struck his brother, and threw the Lady Maud into the river. Too late he learned of her innocence. The stricken men fled—the Earl to the wars again, and execution; his brother to France, where he died of grief. Some said that the Lady Maud's slanderer, overcome by remorse, entered a monastery and was buried in the chancel

at Kempsford. They said, too, that the ghost of the Lady Maud
was seen at night, walking on the water. And this I have written
beside that water, where the pathway is still called Lady Maud's
Walk.

It is unlikely that Shakespeare saw Kempsford, and impossible
that John of Gaunt should have seen Shakespeare, yet when Gaunt
himself thought of Kempsford and the surrounding countryside,
he may well have uttered, in halting prose, the great love song
which Shakespeare spoke for him in poetry:

> This happy breed of men, this little world . . .
> This blessed plot, this earth, this realm, this England.

Another medieval home, long since decayed, gave its name to
the next village, Castle Eaton, which happens to be my own
favourite among the riverside places above Lechlade: not because
it is outstandingly beautiful (the church cannot be compared with
Kempsford's) nor because it was the scene of some classic event,
but because it blends with the river to achieve "a sweet especial
rural scene". Unlike Kempsford, this is a hamlet rather than a
village; and it contains no ugly new house. The only blemish is the
bridge (1895).

Castle Eaton was the *ea-tun* (or place beside a river) with a
castle. It is best viewed from the far side of the river, two hundred
yards away. Here you see an inn whose garden trickles to the
water, and is made colourfully melic by ducks, geese, hens, cows,
and a pig which, since it greets me whenever I pass this way, must
be either very old, or some other pig, or Plato's prototype of
piggery, the Ideal Pig, come down from Eternity expressly to
confute the Logical Positivists. Behind the inn a few old homes
look good to live in, and very likely are so, because none ever
seems to be for sale.

But the loveliest vista lies a few hundred yards down-stream
where the church asserts itself from a mound among trees above
the water. It contains a Norman font, carved by a Thames mason
in the years when the Zouche family built their castle here; a
Tudor pulpit; parts of the medieval rood screen; a medieval
Sanctus bell, set in a turret of slates; and a small chapel to commemorate the men and women who died in war that we might
live at peace.

At Medmenham the river overheard its first country talk,

announcing that London lay astern. At Castle Eaton the talk declares that the west country waits ahead and all around. As France was once divided into *Langue d'oil* and *Langue d'oc* (according as the people pronounced the Roman word for "yes"), so the west of England may be divided into *Langue d'u* and *Langue d'oo* (according as the people pronounce the word "you"). Until the end of the middle ages the men who lived along the Buckinghamshire Thames spoke a dialect that would have been difficult to understand by men living along the Wiltshire Thames, and almost incomprehensible to the riverfolk below Wapping. For example, when Caxton sat down to translate into English a French paraphrase of a Latin poem, he consoled himself by recalling that problems of communication were not confined to literary men: ". . . certain merchaunts," he wrote, "were in a shippe for Tamyse, for to haue sayled ouer the see into Selande, and for lack of wynde thei taryed atte North Forlond [in Kent], and wente to lande for to refresh them; and one of them named Sheffielde, a mercer, cam into an howse and axed for meyte: and specyally axed after eggys: and the good wyf answerde that she coude speke no frenshe. And the marchaunte was angry, for he also coude speke no frenshe, but wolde have hadde *egges* and she understood him not. And theene at laste another sayd he woulde have *eyren* then the good wyf sayd she vnderstood hym wel." That happened towards the end of the fifteenth century. If, towards the end of the twentieth century, an old Tynesider and an old Cornishman sat down together in the tap room at Castle Eaton, they—and the audience with them—might utter the bewildered postscript with which Caxton ended his narrative: "Loo, what sholde a man in thyse days now wryte—*egges* or *eyren?*"

And not only the human voice has changed; the river itself sings a new song because it assumes a new look. Below Great Marlow it flowed unimpeded between locks; even at Eynsham it had only to brush aside Gilbert White's reeds; but above Lechlade no barber trims the banks. Cows create their own ford, slithering through mud, or crumbling a summer dust. Trees die of old age, and are buried down-stream, where they collect twigs and fleece and straw. As a result, the river's "standard" tone—of traffic, weir, silence—gives way to a vernacular of gobbling, sighing, splashing.

Few folk fish hereabouts, and nobody boats, except once in a lifetime, like the two small boys whom we shall presently hear about. All you do see is an unpeopled panorama studded by trees so planted or otherwise sprung-up that they achieve Marvell's "sweet disorder". And amid such sights, accompanied by kindred sounds, the childish Thames splashes past Castle Eaton, lowering its banks, shedding some of its trees, though the aspens abide, like the snow-posts which point a course for wintry travellers across Stainmoor.

This is otters' country, though the otters are hard to find because they build their holts secretively, often under the roots of a tree. Otters observe no specific breeding season, but will move from region to region, more active at night than during the day. Only once during the past eleven years have I seen an otter near the Thames, and that was at Ashton Keynes, where some fish bones guided me to a holt. After several minutes an otter popped up and then plunged down, quick as an eyelid. But Robert of Cricklade must have seen beavers when he lived hereabouts eight hundred years ago, for Wiltshire was a county of beavers, as its place-names testify: Beaverbrook, Beaver Close, Beverly.

Here, if you wish, you may add a second river to your string by tracing the source of a stream which presently gets itself known as Bide Mill Brook, and thereafter joins the Thames at Upper Inglesham.

The Thames itself, meanwhile, has looped so many loops that, in an effort to unravel itself, it dives due south for a mile or so, and then due west, as though intent to climb Hailstone Hill. I like the name Hailstone Hill. It makes me wonder whose bald pate first coined such down-to-earth lyricism. Or was it a shaggy-haired shepherd who shook himself dry in the pub at Cricklade five centuries ago, muttering "Them 'ailstones on that bloody 'ill..."?

The hill, at all events, emphasises a notable feature of the portrait; its dearth of sheer flatness. I cannot recall any reach of the river above Boulter's Lock that is not within sight of rising ground. Here, certainly, the fields within a few yards of the Thames climb to nearly three hundred feet. Further yet, at Blunsdon, they reach almost five hundred feet, which is high ground indeed for southern England.

It is at this point—at any rate in my own experience—that the traveller becomes aware that rivers, like Time itself, are not eternal. Although the narrowing course excites him because it heralds the climax of his journey, it also saddens him because he had come to love this unknown stream and its hinterland of pastoral seclusion. There is (he has discovered) continuous hard work in these parts, but no trace of industry. Shortly before the 1914 War one riverside farmer ploughed her own fields (with a bull alongside a horse) and did most of her own sowing, reaping, and threshing. Here you will find what a Spanish ambassador found long ago: "A clean air, a rosey people, and the river all this while a pleasant stream."

And so to Cricklade, the last small town upon the Thames. One would like to know whether Robert Canutus came by water when he visited his old home. Robert of Cricklade, as the chroniclers called him, was a travelled man who visited Italy, stayed at Canterbury (where he was "many times a loving pilgrim to the holy Archbishop Thomas"), and thereafter became Prior of St. Frideswide's and Chancellor of the University of Oxford. He wrote a life of Becket, in Latin; and Becket's medieval fame is proven by the fact that we know of Robert's biography only from a reference to it in the Icelandic *Thomas Saga*. Another of Robert's works was a translation of Pliny's *Natural History* which he presented to Henry II . . . a royal posey (as Fuller gracefully observed) culled from the finest flowers.

In the parish of Cricklade, at a place named Bradon, stood the Gospel Oak, formerly known as Augustine's because the Saint was said to have sat beneath it while conferring with the Welsh bishops. Not all legends are fictitious, and this legend may record a fact, for the second chapter of the second book of Bede's *A History Of The English Church And People* opens as follows: "Meantime, helped by King Ethelbert, Augustine summoned the bishops . . . to a conference at a place which the English still call Augustine's Oak, on the border between the Hwiccas and the West Saxons."

Some of Cricklade's other legends do not invite acceptance. For instance, Brutus of Troy was said to have founded a university here, in the year 1180 B.C.: and a successor to it was supposed to have been founded in A.D. 950 by Penda, King of Mercia; and thereafter translated into Oxford by Alfred the Great, whom University College once claimed as its founder. The records, by contrast, prove that the real founder of University College was William, Archdeacon of Durham, who in 1249 bequeathed 310 marks, with which the University purchased what is now University College. But legend dies hard, even among scholars. In 1872 the Fellows of University College invited the Regius Professor of History to join the celebrations of their alleged thousandth anniversary. The Professor declined, but showed his interest by enclosing a burned cake.

Yet Cricklade need not rely on legend, for it retains part of the preceptory which the Knights Hospitallers built; and from Henry II the townsfolk received an unusual privilege, in recognition of their kindness to Henry's mother, the Empress Matilda, who in 1139 came to England to claim the Throne. Matilda, wife of the Emperor Henry V, was the daughter of Henry I; her rival, Stephen of Blois, was Henry's nephew. In the anarchy which followed, Cricklade suffered so severely that its plunderers were named by the chroniclers; but the townsfolk, despite their tribulations, received the Empress kindly when she sought refuge from her enemies, and that is why her son allowed Cricklade men to sell their goods exempt from market dues throughout the kingdom. They still enjoy that right.

Even more remarkable is the Court Leet, which at Cricklade has continued since the Middle Ages. It was allowed to lapse during recent years, but still retains its ancient jurisdiction.

Cricklade has two churches. The smaller, St. Mary's, contains a chained Bible; the larger is dedicated to St. Samson of Dol (Dol-de-Bretagne), who symbolized the affinities between the Celtic fisherfolk of Brittany and their Cornish cousins. Samson, in fact, crossed the Channel in order to convert the pagan Cornish; and at Bodmin (they tell) he found some of them worshipping "an abominable image, on a hill-top". This abomination was very likely no more desolate than any other of the granite boulders on Bodmin Moor; but Samson took no chances. Having destroyed the stone—a feat worthy of his eyeless namesake—he set a cross on another stone. A thirteenth-century window in the church contains some modern glass showing, among others, St. Dubrivius, by whom St. Samson was ordained. The lordly tower was built by John Dudley, Duke of Northumberland. Like St. Mary's, this church has a medieval stone cross near the entrance.

The original rectorial endowment was a small Parsonage farm adjoining the church, which has been allowed to fall to bits. The

Parsonage barn was a masterpiece, ninety-two feet long by twenty-four feet wide, built by the masons, smiths, and carpenters of Cricklade. It was demolished in 1964.

The port of Cricklade probably stood to the north of the medieval town wall, having a wharf on each side of the Thames, and a cause-way linking it with the Ermine Street to Cirencester, which was a supply settlement, *Corinium*, next after *Londinium* the largest city in Roman Britain. A Roman gravestone of the third century was found at Cricklade, with sherds, coins, bricks, tiles, and a bronze statuette. The name Cricklade was originally *criccagelad*, meaning "the place with wharves or creeks, where the river can be crossed".

At Cricklade the river is best seen by following Thames Lane into a farmyard, at which point the river is beyond dispute a stream. An athlete could jump across it. Very slowly it flows, very winding, but still accompanied by the trees that have kept the promise made at Teddington. Beyond Cricklade it bears north-north-west towards the high land of Duke's Brake. Alongside Hailstone Hill and the old canal it swerves south before settling south-west into Ashton Keynes. At this stage the traveller may easily follow a stream which seems to be the Thames, but is not. East of Cricklade flows the Derry Brook, and alongside it a stream so small that nobody has bothered to call it anything at all. Beyond them is the River Churn, and beyond that the old Canal. Eastward again run the River Ray and a second stream too small to have been baptized. Southward you see the River Key. And each of these is capable of passing itself off as any of the others. Defoe faced a similar dilemma three centuries ago: "In passing this way," he wrote, "we very remarkably crossed four rivers . . . and enquiring their name, the country people call'd them every one the Thames."

This particular ignorance has its general counterpart, for the infant Thames seems altogether to have escaped the notice of great literature. Certainly no one has praised it as Wordsworth praised the River Duddon in his native Lakeland. Yet this is no mean river, even in its infancy. At times it can startle, as when the few feet of August water dwindle until the river bed appears, cracked like parched lips. Then the fag-ends chucked by farmfolk are hulks left high and dry (though February would have swirled them down-stream at eight knots). Sometimes a

lizard crawls where minnows used to leap; and cows stare bewildered at their withered Thames. The river itself dies of thirst,
and its death-bed is painted by one line of Leconte de Lisle:
". . . *la source est tardie où bouvaient les troupeaux* . . ."

An even fiercer struggle for existence will occur in winter,
when you can stand at Waterhay Bridge, between Cricklade and
Ashton Keynes, while a gale bends the elms ominously. Even the
willows bend, taut as bows. The cows, weary of failing to find
shelter, stand udder-deep in flooded fields. The Thames is
invisible, as it was during the drought, though this time drowned
in its own excesses.

The flora and fauna, on the other hand, are less startling. Otters
are dwindling, beavers dead; even the herons wane. Nor has the
Thames anything with which to surprise a botanist. Even so, the
meadows around Cricklade yield their quota of flowers, not the
less beautiful for being common . . . marsh-marigolds, water-
crowfoot, yellow water-lily, buttercups, primroses, celandines,
John Clare's "sweet grass" or meadow hay. And, of course, farms
and cottages paint their own time of year with snowdrops, hollyhocks, and winter jasmine. Above all, and despite the times, this
riverscape remains as peaceful as the Duddon's which Wordsworth praised two centuries ago, "remote from every taint of
sordid industry". One sees beside the Thames now what Wordsworth saw beside the Duddon then:

> Hail to the fields—with dwellings sprinkled o'er,
> And one small hamlet, under a green hill
> Clustering, with barn and byre, and spouting mill.

South of Waterhay Bridge, three narrow lanes converge on
Leigh, where the land is three hundred feet high. One wonders
why the villagers did not build their thirteenth-century church
there, instead of leaving it lower down, at the mercy of the floods.
During the nineteenth century the villagers amended that mistake.
They demolished their church, and then rebuilt it on higher
ground. They took down the great door, with the nails which a
Leigh farmer had forged for it. They took the belfry, the font,
the fragments of medieval glass. But one thing they left behind—
the chancel. That remained where it was placed, but no longer as
it was built; only the skeleton survived, melancholy even on a
summer day.

From Leigh to Aston Keynes is not much above a mile, and there the Thames is joined by the Swillbrook, which has itself received so many brooklets that its name connotes a species rather than a specimen.

At Ashton Keynes the houses on one side of the street are old and therefore handsome; and since the river divides them from the road, each has its own footbridge which, in the words of John of Gaunt of Kempsford:

> . . . serves it in the office of a wall,
> Or as a moat defensive to a house.

Yet these bridges could act against the interest of the householder who had taken more than enough ale for his stomach's sake. Did not an eminent sixteenth-century physiologist, Thomas Willis, say of himself, that "after an extra good bout of wine he could see to read print clearly on a very dark night"? Willis may have been right, but the older villagers will tell you of revellers who were more often wrong, and had to be fished from the stream. What an unnecessary pity, that this village has been marred by two garages, each succeeding in looking the uglier.

Nowhere in Ashton Keynes is the river more than ten feet wide, yet a considerable volume of river traffic came here, almost within living memory. Why has a navigable fairway dwindled into a narrow stream? The chief reason is the railway and the car which caused people to neglect the river. But centuries of felling must have played their part by reducing the density of foliage and therewith the condensation of moisture for springs. Private hatches and impromptu weirs also impeded a free passage.

Ashton Keynes has the base of four medieval crosses, which prove that the village has dwindled as sharply as its river. Cobbett, who came here in 1826, emphasized the decline in four words: formerly, he wrote, it was "a large market town". Standing here today it is impossible to believe that Ashton Keynes once bustled with barges, pack-horses, wagons, and bundle-bowed pedlars. Yet one clue does exist, in the name of the General Stores, which is called London House; that being the old name for shops selling the best quality of goods.

The church of this village of crosses was dedicated to the Holy Cross. It stands at the end of an avenue of limes, having the base of one of its four crosses near the entrance. It is transitional-Norman, with twelfth-century font, thirteenth-century arches, fourteenth-century gargoyles.

There was a monastery here, long since decayed. A farmhouse on the site may have been part of the monks' domestic quarters. You can still see what may be the remains of a monastic moat in the meadows nearby.

Just as Old Shifford was a pioneer among English nonconformists, so this reach of the river was a pioneer among English Moravians. At the nearby village of Tytherton a certain John Cennick, whom Wesley chose as the first of his lay preachers, built a Methodist Chapel. Cennick, however, broke from Methodism, and converted his chapel into a Moravian church. Some of the Ashton Keynes people still are Moravians. Their sect has more than 100,000 members throughout the world, each church sending a bishop to an ecumenical synod every ten years. England and Wales contain nearly three thousand Moravians and their Moravian pastors. They are a missionizing sect, maintaining cordial relations with Anglicanism and Methodism. Moravianism itself began in or about the year 1467 as a handful of Protestants who spread from Czecho-Slovakia into Poland. It was at a Moravian meeting in Aldersgate Street that John Wesley received the call to evangelicalism, at the moment when, in his own words, "one was reading Luther's preface to the Romans".

By this time the explorer has already confronted a cardinal difficulty: if he wishes to follow the river, or even to catch sight of it, he can do so only by trespassing. Trespass is a matter for lawyers, of whom I am not one, but a few homely facts may seem helpful. First, do not be deterred by signs saying Trespassers Will Be Prosecuted. Trespassers will not be prosecuted. Only the Crown can prosecute the wrongdoer. Trespass is not a crime; it is a civil offence, for which the offender is liable to be, not prosecuted by the Crown, but sued by a subject. A landowner may ask a trespasser to leave his property; and, if the trespasser refuses to leave, the owner may lawfully eject him by using reasonable force. By and large, the Courts will not punish a trespasser who has damaged nothing, stolen nothing, and generally conducted himself in an orderly manner. In all my years of wandering beside the Thames I have never met a landowner who objected to me walking through his fields.

Above Cricklade this matter of trespass becomes urgent because the river repeatedly retreats in order to advance. For the religious and the military such tactics often achieve their objective, but even the hardiest walker must weary of following a course three times longer than the meadow which it crosses.

A strictly legal solution of the matter is simple; having discovered (if you can) the name and address of every landowner en route, you obtain their permission to follow the river yard by yard. That leaves only the act of following it, which would be simple were it not difficult, for the Thames above Ashton Keynes burrows through so many copses, among such irritable briars, that a walker, if he is to emerge unscathed, must swaddle himself into a composite bee-keeper, furze-cutter, and hip-high-trout-tickler. This precept of perfection I tried and long ago discarded. Few farmers have either the time or the inclination to explain where their property meets another's. So now I walk as I please, obtaining permission when it is easily obtainable, avoiding gardens, crops, gates marked BULL (these usually enclose a maiden heifer, or may even have been altered from PULL) and generally respecting all those privacies which only a Marxist would regard as public.

Meanwhile the infant Thames has flowed past several of its features—two water-mills in as many miles, and a Wick that was once a dairy-farm.

There follow some three miles of companionable solitude, skirting villages that have much to say for themselves . . . Somerford Keynes, for example, which in 1212 was held by William de Kaines, a Norman. Somerford means what it says—a place where the river can be forded in summer. This may have been the highest ford on the Thames. An avenue of elms leads the way towards a Tudor manor house flanked by trim lawns, and graced by yet another Thames dove-cote—gabled and mullioned. I came here once on a summer morning, when the house was unoccupied, except by the generations who had once lived there, and were acknowledged by a line of Walter de la Mare:

There haunts in Time's bare house an active ghost.

The church is hidden among limes, firs, beeches, chestnuts. Its north wall has a blocked Saxon porch and a segment of Saxon carving, showing the heads of two terrifying animals. In the aisle is a marble effigy of Robert Strange, a sixteenth-century lord of the manor, accompanied by two skulls—a double *memento mori* for the living. Two windows commemorate Christopher Fawcett and his son, William, who were vicars here for ninety years. Ten Somerford Keynes men died during the World Wars, and are remembered by a memorial showing St. George slaying the dragon.

Near Somerford Keynes the river passes the last (or first) of its water-mills (the wheel was demolished at the end of the nineteenth century). The farm called Upper Mill Farm was the highest on the Thames.

South Cerney, a mile or two away, is worth visiting, if only because the name Cerney is a corruption of Churn, a tributary of the Thames. This village remains relatively unspoiled. Its Cotswold houses and the thatched cottages are well-tended. A Norman church contains fragments of a twelfth century timber crucifix, once painted and still showing traces of colour. Anne Edwards was buried here. During the last century she built, at the north end of the village, an almshouse for widows and orphans of clergy in the diocese of Gloucester. Few other churches have memorials to a brace of centenarians—Walter Porlock of the eighteenth century and Anne Billiard of the twentieth.

In this part of the Thames country the craft of glove-making used to flourish. A few old people still remember seeing their mother sewing gloves at home. Glove-making was revived during the 1920s, but never again as a cottage craft.

Another feature of the portrait hereabouts is the vivid soil, for this is Cotswold country. Many people assume that the word Cotswold means "wolds" containing "cots". This is not so. In 1250 the name was spelled as *Coteswaud* meaning "the *wald* or forest belonging to Cod": *Cod* being a chieftain who is recorded at the Worcestershire village of Cutsdean, formerly *Codestune* or *Cod's tun*.

Although the phrase "Cotswold country" is commonly used to describe a hilly region of Oxfordshire and Gloucestershire, it would be more properly used to define a type of stone that is found in parts of Warwickshire, Oxfordshire, Gloucestershire, Worcestershire and Wiltshire. This rock is Oolite (from two Greek words meaning "egg" and "stone"), and its name is another example of homely baptism because "Cotswold stone" is composed of lumps of egg-shaped calcium carbonate which do resemble a fish's roe. Oolite is of two kinds, Inferior and Great; the former coming from a lower stratum, the latter being the more vivid—sometimes almost as bright as an orange.

Generally—though not always—new houses in the Cotswolds must be built of Cotswold stone. They weather well, and within ten years have acquired a venerable complexion. Together with the Cotswold churches they form an indigenously local feature of the portrait, and are by-products of a cycle which the north-countryman calls "from grass to brass". The rock, in short, yields a soil of rich herbage; the herbage yields a harvest of prime meat and fleece; these yield a corresponding harvest of "brass" or money, with which our forefathers built their churches, manors, farmhouses, cottages. So it may be said that the Thames has three distinctive styles of architecture—the red-brick houses of Berkshire, the Chilterns' brick-and-flint cottages, and these beautiful Cotswold homes.

By this time the Thames has become not so much difficult to follow as hard to find. A number of brooks and dykes appear, too small to be shown on the one-inch Ordnance Survey map. Local people tell a tale about a London photographer who gave the riverfolk a lecture on this reach of the Thames, illustrated by photographs which he had taken especially for the occasion. Not until his lecture ended did the cameraman discover that he had been talking about the Thames while showing pictures of the Churn.

As though to baffle visitors, the Thames above Somerford Keynes bisects itself, merges again at Upper Mill Farm, and once more bisects itself until, at a small wood on the outskirts of Ewen, it agrees that the Both ought to be the One.

Ewen is a scattering of ancient homes and a Cotswold stone inn, "The Wild Duck" (disfigured by some Edwardian street gas-lamps). At "The Wild Duck" Cornelius Uzzle (he ought to have been Guzzle) publically and for profit consumed twelve pounds of bacon, half of it raw, the remainder boiled. It may be said of Cornelius Uzzle what Jack Falstaff remarked of himself: ". . . a goodly portly man, i'faith, and a corpulent. . . ." Like Ewelme, Ewen takes its name from the Old English *aewielm*, meaning either "a spring" (as at Ewelme) or "the source of a river" (as at Ewen).

The Thames does not enter Ewen, but flows to the south of it, dividing once more into two parts, then crossing under the road from Kemble to South Cerney, past high and wooded country, notably between Kemble Wood and Jackament's Bottom, where the hills are not far short of five hundred feet.

Kemble, too, the river by-passes, though only by a few hundred yards. The village is bisected by the road. Its better half lies south of that road; the worse is hotch-potched with modern houses. Kemble contains two curios: the first is a yew tree whose trunk has been pierced to reveal another tree growing inside; the second is the south transept of the church, which was carried from a chapel-of-ease at Ewen, within Kemble parish, and re-assembled as replica of its former self. A man at "The Wild Duck" assured me that for many years the baptismal font had been used as a feeding trough.

Near Kemble the river follows the road, being in some places less than three feet wide. The child, said Wordsworth, is father to the man; and Father Thames at Kemble is indeed a child . . . less than a child . . . a helpless infant. It talks to itself and occasionally wets itself (and the fields also). It requires of us those services which it cannot perform. Many times I have lugged a fallen bough from the banks, or fished-up leaves that were impeding its passage.

So far astern as Kelmscot the houses announced a Cotswold country, but at Kemble the very essence and texture of the Cotswolds appear—the hills—uprising like fruitful ramparts. At Hailey Wood they are six hundred feet high; at Chalford, away to the west, they are not far short of a thousand feet. As among the Chilterns, the air is perennially fresh; the sky unenclosed; the earth beneath it a mosaic, the same that Gerard Manley Hopkins painted:

> Landscape plotted and pieced—fold, fallow, plough;
> And all trades, their gear and tackle and trim.

Ploughs, indeed, take the place of people. Sometimes they seek the shelter of a hedge. Sometimes they muse in mid-field, stiller than scarecrows. Sometimes they drone into the distance, slow as a wintry fly pacing the same impenetrable pane. High, wide, and handsome . . . the phrase takes on a new and indigenous timbre. When Goring is glutted, and Lechlade loud with summer tourists, this countryside keeps quiet all day, carrying only enough cars to heighten the silence. At Cricklade I have swum in luxurious privacy. At Ashton Keynes I have basked full-length in clear water. Even at Ewen I have splashed and paddled. Now, at Kemble, the river is too narrow even for paddling. The skyline hills announce that our journey is nearly ended.

But the source of the Thames lies this side of those hills, and it seems impossible that this trickle of water could have tottered from more than a few hundred yards away. Looking down at it, one says what the man said in H. G. Wells's novel: ". . . is this little wet ditch the Historical River Thames?"

XV

ALPHA AND OMEGA:
KEMBLE TO THAMES HEAD

THIS little wet ditch is indeed "the historical River Thames", and it does manage to totter for more than a few hundred yards.

Half-a-mile north-east of Kemble it flows under a disused railway, past a disused canal, and thence under the Fosse Way by Thames Head Bridge, the highest on the river. Many conscientious explorers come this way, and fail to find any stream at all. During prolonged drought even its course is hard to find. Beyond Thames Head Bridge the one-inch Ordnance map ceases to mark the river.

This evident invisibility has caused some people to doubt whether Thames Head really is the source. Certainly it seems strange that the beginnings of Britain's premier river were not discovered and long ago proclaimed beyond dispute. Even had it been impossible to confirm an undoubted wellspring, the experts might reasonably have been expected to create a geological fiction by selecting one probable source, and agreeing to abide by it. But no such unanimity was achieved. At least two places claim to be the source; and John Masefield once told me that the Welsh used to co-opt the Thames into Cymry, saying that it arose among their own hills, and entered England by flowing underneath the Severn. I have yet to meet the geologist who accepted that hypothesis. It echoes too loudly the pride of Owen Glendower, who boasted that he could divert the River Trent: "I can call spirits from the vasty deep" . . . to which Harry Hotspur, a mere Englishman, retorted:

> Why, so can I, or so can any man;
> But will they come when you do call for them?

The text of *Henry The Fourth* reveals that Glendower returned an evasive answer.

Many Thamesfolk believed—and a few still do believe—that the river rises at Seven Springs near Cheltenham, where a stone bears an inscription: *Hic Tuus O Tamisine Pater Septemgeminus Fons*. But Seven Springs is simply a tributary of a tributary, the River Churn, which joins the Thames near Cricklade, several miles away. Every geologist with whom I have discussed the problem agreed that Thames Head is the true source. Camden thought so, Leland thought so; the Ordnance Survey and the Thames Conservators continue to think so. Thames Head is certainly the pleasanter site.

Although the source of the Thames has ceased to be a matter of serious dispute, no one has felt that it was necessary to offer any form of guidance for pilgrims travelling to the source of our foremost river. The best landmark is an inn on the far side of the Fosse Way, about a mile west of Thames Head Bridge, and about three miles west of Cirencester. Formerly The Railway Inn, this gaily hospitable tavern became The Thames Head Inn during the 1960s. From it you must follow the main road northeast for perhaps five hundred yards, where an un-posted lane leads leftward from a cottage. It is an inviting lane flanked by trees and dry-stone walls. Some six hundred yards along it, on the left, you will see a gate. You must pass through this gate and across a meadow. No public right of way exists, but, as at Kempsford, the landowner is a generous host. At the far end of his meadow you will meet a track which enters a sheltered hollow. And there rises the River Thames.

The site used to be marked by a twentieth-century monument in the eighteenth-century manner (erected by the Thames Conservators), showing Father Thames plumply yet discreetly unattired, holding a home-made canoe-paddle which, one feels, was not part of the original design, but rather an after-thought by pilgrims. The statue now stands at St. John's Lock, Lechlade.

At the foot of this monument someone had assembled a small pile of stones, as though to pin-point the wellspring. Throughout most of the year, however, the stones are as dry as the proverbial bone. Only after heavy rainfall does the spring appear. Occasionally—perhaps thrice in a lifetime—the rain is heavy enough to cause severe flooding. Then the guidebooks are confounded by their assertion that the Thames above Cricklade is un-navigable. Such a flood occurred during the 1960s, enabling two boys to canoe down-stream from the source. That is not an old wives' tale. I have seen newspaper pictures of the boys, paddling their craft within a few feet of the monument.

As with Stonehenge, so at Thames Head—some people come here and are disappointed. They had expected a second Cliveden or another Goring. One may understand their disappointment without sharing it. The country hereabouts is good plain Englishry which is another way of saying that it is beautiful. No traffic disturbs Thames Head, no road: only the hills, a cottage hidden in a copse, and that harmony of breeze, bird-song, and sheep which we call silence. The Thames, in fact, is born at home, as it were in a cottage, with the birds and the cattle and the farmfolk all about. At this remote place the beginning is also an end, from which you look back upon the voyage; with the mind's eye examining again whatever most impressed you by the way. Thames Head, in short, is numinous, for here began and hither returns the mainstream of English history.

From these skies, in this field, were distilled the waters which Caesar crossed; which saw the rise and watched the fall of castles and abbeys and dynasties; which swept king-makers and king-destroyers under Traitors Gate; which slapped De Ruyter when, with a broom for ensign, he led his Dutchmen up the Thames, and shivered Parliament with salvos; which carried a goodly part of the commerce of the world's richest merchant; which quenched the flames unleashed by Hitler; which nourished both the substance and the spirit of innumerable men and women, unknown in their own day, and to this age less than nameless.

And to a general litany will be added those particular memories which each man nurtures according to his taste . . . Traherne of Teddington, reborn at a London bookstall; the great Garrick, no longer a Lear, but a man-about-the-house, planting next summer's roses; the duel in the woods above Cliveden, and a woman watching while the lover kills a husband; The Royal Swans of Cookham, the private aisle at Mapledurham, William Morris working his tapestries at Kelmscot, the Romans building their wharves at Cricklade. The list is legion, and for an evocation of it and of Thames Head, what finer than the man who was born near the Gloucestershire Thames at Down Ampney—Ralph Vaughan Williams and his *Lark Ascending*. For the Thames also is ascending, rising up tremulously from the earth, flowing forward to a future, though its landfall is less predictable—even, indeed, less imaginable—than in the years when a butcher's boy was rowed from Hampton Court Palace, with a Cardinal's hat on his head, and in his hand the destiny of Europe. No man can foresee what men will become; whether conditioned robots, or emigrants who made a new life upon another star, leaving this one unpeopled, and the rivers thereof to their own devices. But a future there will be, and who shall deny that in it the Thames may play some part in the life of another Shakespeare and of a second Churchill?

The history of a nation can resemble the course of a river; lagging sometimes in sluggish shallows; sometimes seeming to be parched; yet recovering and proceeding; drawing indeed upon its past, but always moving forward. England has not run dry, nor will she fail, while there are men who practise their belief that the Thames shall one day flow into a sea of pure goodwill, where the Amazon and the Danube and the Volga and the Nile bear each their own proud heritage, not with malice, but of loving-kindness.

THAMES HEAD

Father of English Rivers, here the Thames
In swaddling clothes, or as it were a bird
Poised for its fledgling flight, from this field stems
With childhood's babbling innocence: then is heard
Maturity and manhood's clash of arms
Arrayed against itself and half the world;
A roll-call of excursion and alarms
Gone to the wars again, with flag unfurled.
But that was only part, and not the most;
This river is its people and their home;
A myriad and multifarious host
Intent as bees above the honeycomb.
From this, their field, these infant waters run
Toward the Father that was once a son.

INDEX

A

Abingdon, 128–30
Aelfric, 129, 153
Albert Bridge, 45
Alfred, King, 160, 164, 185
Alice, Duchess of Suffolk, 117–18, 156
Anne, Queen, 18, 28
Appleford, 126
Appleton, 157, 159
Ascham, Robert, 68
Ashbrook, Viscount, 158
Ashton Ferry, 74
Ashton Keynes, 188–90
Asquith and Oxford, Earl of, 127

B

Bablock Hythe, 155, 156, 157
Bacon, Roger, 141–2
Balliol College, 36, 136, 139, 143
Bampton, 148, 159, 161–2
Basildon, 53, 108
Battersea, 14
Beaumont College, 40
Bede, 25, 122, 185
Belloc, Hilaire, 136, 162
Bensington, 116
Billingsgate, 44
Binsey, 143–4, 148
Bisham, 16, 65, 67
Bishop, John, 64
Blackfriars Bridge, 21
Blackmore, R. D., 25, 33, 147
Blackstone, Sir William, 114
Blanche, Duchess of Lancaster, 180
Blount, family, 98–100
Blunt, Wilfred, 110

Boethius, 68
Bonner, Bishop, 46
Boswell, James, 139, 143
Bourne End, 63
Boulters Lock, 54, 59, 66
Boveney Loch, 49
Bradford Brook, 113
Brasenose College, 24, 139
Bray, 20, 50–1, 84, 92
Bridges, Robert, 48, 106–7, 145, 171
Bridgman, Sir Orlando, 24
Bridgewater, Duke of, 95
Brindley, James, 95, 142
Brontë, Emily, 132
Brown, Capability, 30, 133
Brown, Thomas, 149
Browne, Sir Thomas, 13, 14
Brooke, W. T., 24
Brunel, Sir Isambard Kingdom, 52–3, 108, 112, 142
Bunyan, John, 179
Buscot, 167–8
Bushy Park, 25, 26
Butt, Dame Clara, 112

C

Caesar, Julius, 17, 25, 32, 198
Camberwell, 30
Cambrensis, Giraldus, 85
Camden, William, 123, 177, 197
Camoys, Lord, 79
Campbell, Squire, 167–8
Campion, Edmund, 80
Carlyle, Thomas, 20, 95
Cardigan, Lord, 77
Castle Eaton, 182–3